HISTORY-SOCIAL SCIENCE FOR CALIFORNIA
OUR COMMUNITIES

WILLIAM E. WHITE, Ph.D.
PROGRAM AUTHOR

PEARSON

Scott
Foresman

EDITORIAL OFFICES
Glenview, Illinois
Parsippany, New Jersey
New York, New York

SALES OFFICES
Needham, Massachusetts
Duluth, Georgia
Glenview, Illinois
Coppell, Texas
Sacramento, California
Mesa, Arizona

ISBN: 0-328-16671-5

Contents

A Book About Our Communities

Do you ever wonder what the area where you live was like years ago? Do you think it looked different than it does now? Have the people and buildings changed?

This book is *your* book. It is about the many areas of our state, including yours. It is about how some things have changed in these places, while other things have stayed the same over time. Just like the area where you live, your book is special in many ways.

Camarillo many years ago

Silicon Valley today

First, you will write, circle, and underline words in your book. You will also fill in time lines and draw on maps.

Second, every unit in your book begins with a Study Journal. You will write about what you already know about your community. You will also write what you learn on these pages.

Finally, you will find many photographs and drawings of people and places in our communities. Some pictures will show things from the past. Others will show how things look today.

What You Will Learn

Your book begins by describing the land and water in different areas of California. For example, some areas have mountains, while others have deserts. Different kinds of plants and animals also live in these places. People have learned to use things in their area to make what they need to live.

You will learn that California Indians were the first people to live in California. They had different ways of life based on the different features in their area. California Indians used what they found to make food, homes, clothes, and tools. Some California Indians still follow their way of life from years ago. But they have changed how they live in other ways.

Many other people moved to California during our state's history. They are still coming here today. These people traveled from many other states and other countries. They came here for different reasons. Some came to explore. Some worked on the railroad. Some were searching for gold. They started new lives and began businesses in different parts of California. Some of these businesses are still here today.

Some people from Europe first sailed along the coast of present-day California in the 1500s.

California Indians have used materials in their area to make things that they need, such as this basket.

Dancers celebrate the Mexican holiday of Cinco de Mayo in Los Angeles.

Overview • **v**

How do the many people who have come to California get along? They agree on certain rules that help them live and work together. These rules might be about safety, fairness, or taking care of California's land and water. You will read about the people who help run our neighborhoods, our state, and our country.

Even though the area where we live has many products and services that make our lives better, we still need things from other places. You will learn how the people of California work with each other and with people outside our state and country to get the things we need.

These students are listening to a California Indian storyteller.

The Next Step

Are you ready to learn more about where you live? Do you wonder what has changed over the years or what has stayed the same? As you read, you will begin to understand what California was like in the past. You will see how some things have changed and how others have remained the same. Turn the page to begin your trip into the story of *Our Communities.*

Study Journal

In this unit you will learn about the features of the land in your area and other areas of California. You will learn how people have used the land to meet their needs. Complete the activities on these pages as you read the unit.

What I know about . . .

California's land:

California's Environment

Shade each region on the map with a different color. Shade the map legend when you are done. Then list one resource from each region.

Coast resource:

Mountain resource:

Valley resource:

Desert resource:

Map Legend

◯ Coast   ◯ Mountain

◯ Valley   ◯ Desert

Complete these sections as you read the unit.

Circle the region of California in which you live. Write three details about its geography.

- Desert
- Coast
- Mountain
- Valley

1.

2.

3.

Draw a picture of a resource in California that needs to be protected. Write a sentence explaining why people should help protect it.

List one detail that tells why the dam and canal are important.

Shasta Dam

Panama Canal

I have learned . . .

Name:

🐻 **H-SS 3.1.2** Trace the ways in which people have used the resources of the local region and modified the physical environment (e.g., a dam constructed upstream changed a river or coastline).

How have people used the land in your region?

CONNECT TO YOU People use things around them to do work and to make useful things. What would you use if you wanted to build a treehouse or grow a plant?

Preview the Lesson

Vocabulary

resource *(n.)* anything that meets people's needs

environment *(n.)* the land, water, and air in which people, animals, and plants live

dam *(n.)* a wall built to hold back water

flood *(n.)* a sudden flow of water that covers what is normally dry land

canal *(n.)* a narrow waterway that has been dug across land

protect *(v.)* to keep someone or something safe

Vocabulary Activity Circle the word above that is a synonym for *watch over* and *look after*.

🔊 **Reading:** Main Idea and Details

The *main idea* tells you what a paragraph is about. *Details* tell you more about the main idea. Underline the details in the paragraph on page 10.

▷

9

Redwood
National Park — Shasta Dam
Los Angeles
Panama
Canal

1907 The Port
of Los Angeles
opens.

1914

Soil, Water, and Forests

California has many different resources.
A **resource** is anything that meets people's
needs. The valley region has rich soil that
makes the area good for growing crops.
Soil is an important resource, as are forests.
Nearly half of our state is covered with
forests. Paper and lumber for houses and
furniture are made from the wood from
forests. Rivers and lakes are resources
too. They give us water for drinking and
growing crops.

1. Main Idea and Details
**Name one of California's
resources. Then explain
its use.**

California's forests, such as Klamath
National Forest (*below*), are one of
our state's many resources.

1945 Shasta Dam is completed.

1968 Redwood National Park opens.

Changing the Land

People can change their environment. The **environment** is the land, water, and air in which people, animals, and plants live. Workers completed Shasta Dam on the Sacramento River in 1945. A **dam** is a wall built to hold back water. Shasta Dam is one of the largest dams in the United States.

Dams, such as Shasta Dam, provide power for electricity and water for growing crops. Dams also can prevent floods by holding river water behind a wall. A **flood** happens when a sudden flow of water covers what is normally dry land.

2. **What might happen if people did not build dams?**

Predict

_____

_____

_____

_____

Work began on Shasta Dam in 1938 and finished in 1945. The dam is made of concrete.

11

Better Travel

People build ports and canals to make it easier to send products by ship. The Port of Los Angeles was opened in 1907 to take in larger ships. Canals can make travel by water faster. A **canal** is a narrow waterway that has been dug across land.

In 1914 workers completed the Panama Canal. The Panama Canal cuts through a strip of land in the country of Panama. This land divides the Atlantic and Pacific Oceans. Ships could sail more quickly between the East and West Coasts of the United States after the Panama Canal was built. The Port of Los Angeles grew larger as a result.

This is how the Port of Los Angeles looks today.

3. How did the Panama Canal help the Port of Los Angeles grow?

Cause and Effect

_____

_____

_____

_____

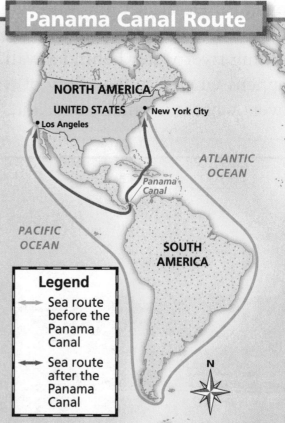

Panama Canal Route

NORTH AMERICA

UNITED STATES · New York City

· Los Angeles

ATLANTIC OCEAN

Panama Canal

PACIFIC OCEAN

SOUTH AMERICA

Legend

⟷ Sea route before the Panama Canal

⟷ Sea route after the Panama Canal

N

This map shows the sea routes before and after the Panama Canal was built. On the map legend, circle the symbol that stands for the shorter route.

A Healthy Environment

Sometimes people change the environment, and that causes problems. For example, people can get sick from pollution. Pollution makes the environment dirty. It makes the air that we breathe or the water that we drink unclean. Many people think it is important to protect our environment. **Protect** means to keep someone or something safe. People can help by following rules that protect the environment.

Many people have worked to protect the environment. John Muir (MYOOR) worked to protect California's resources more than 100 years ago. He made sure that people all over the world knew about our state's beauty. He died in 1914. But his work later helped to create parks such as Redwood National Park, which was established in 1968.

John Muir worked to protect our state's natural beauty.

4. ⟳ Main Idea and Details

Circle one way that people can protect the environment.

California redwoods grow in Muir Woods. The woods were named for John Muir.

Summary

California has many resources. How have people changed the environment to use resources?

Resource Maps

Learn More Resource maps show the resources of an area. California is rich in natural resources. The symbols on the map below stand for our state's many resources. The map legend tells you what the symbols stand for. Find the oranges symbol in the legend. It stands for orange groves, or orange tree farms. The map shows you where California's many orange groves can be found.

Use the map to answer the following questions.

Try It

1. **What are two resources found along or near the coast?** *Identify*

   _____

   _____

2. **Put a box around the region where almonds are grown.** *Identify*

3. **In which half of the state are oranges grown?** *Identify*

   _____

4. **Draw a circle around a resource in your region.** *Apply*

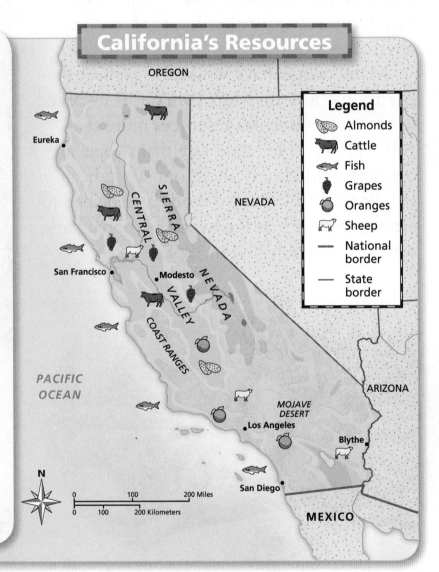

California's Resources

Legend
- Almonds
- Cattle
- Fish
- Grapes
- Oranges
- Sheep
- — National border
- — State border

Study Journal

In this unit you will learn about the California Indian groups that live in your region and other regions. You will find out about the land where they lived, their beliefs, their systems of order, and what happened when they met other people who had come to California. Complete the activities on these pages as you read the unit.

What I know about . . .

California Indian groups:

California Indian Customs

Fill in each circle below with an example of a California Indian custom.

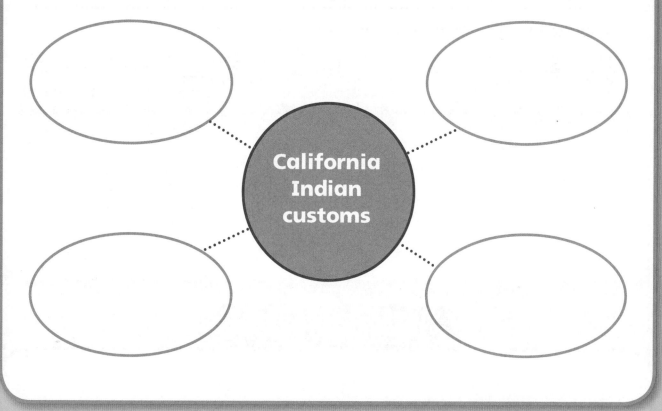

California Indian customs

Complete these sections as you read the unit.

Write one fact about each California Indian group.

Mountain

Valley

Coast

Desert

Choose two words below and write one sentence using both words.

- laws
- economy
- tribal government
- reservation
- constitution

Complete the missing information in the time line below.

1700s	1767	1775

I have learned . . .

H-SS 3.2.1 Describe national identities, religious beliefs, customs, and various folklore traditions.

How are California Indians in your region alike and different?

CONNECT TO YOU

Where did your family come from? They might have come from Asia, Europe, South America, or Africa. American Indians, or Native Americans, were living here long before people from other lands arrived.

Preview the Lesson

Vocabulary

custom *(n.)* a way of doing things

folklore *(n.)* the stories and customs of a group of people

tradition *(n.)* a special way a group of people does something and that has been passed on to others

ceremony *(n.)* an important activity done for a special reason

Vocabulary Activity Circle a word in the list above that could be a synonym for *tradition.*

○ Reading: Compare and Contrast

To *compare* is to tell how two or more things are alike. To *contrast* is to tell how two or more things are different. A common clue word used for things that are alike is *like.* Common clue words for differences are *different, but,* and *however.* Underline these clue words as you read the lesson.

North American Indians

North America was home to many different groups of American Indians before Europeans arrived. Each group had its own **customs,** or ways of doing things. North American Indian groups still have their own customs today.

These American Indian groups spoke different languages, ate different foods, and built different types of homes. American Indians of the Eastern Woodlands planted corn and beans and hunted deer. Some of them built houses called wigwams out of wood and bark. The American Indians of the Great Plains lived in earth lodges most of the time. They hunted buffalo and used buffalo skin for clothing and shelter. Buffalo-skin tepees were used during hunting trips.

Some American Indians of the Desert Southwest lived in stone or clay houses. They grew corn even though there was not much water in the desert. Finding food was not a problem for groups of the Pacific Northwest. They ate a lot of fish and shellfish because they lived near the Pacific Ocean. They also hunted whales and seals in the ocean.

1. Compare and Contrast

List two important differences between American Indians of the Eastern Woodlands and of the Great Plains.

American Indian Groups

PACIFIC NORTHWEST

GREAT PLAINS

EASTERN WOODLANDS

DESERT SOUTHWEST

Circle the name of the American Indian group that hunted buffalo.

California's Indian Groups

California's many Indian groups had different ways of life. Some, like the Modoc, Pomo, and Yuki, lived in northern California. They hunted deer and elk and fished. However, the Chumash lived along the south-central California coast. They mostly ate fish, shellfish, other sea animals, and birds. The Washo lived near Lake Tahoe in the Sierra Nevada. They hunted deer and antelope for food, clothing, and shelter. The Mojave and Yuma lived in the southern desert. They farmed on the dry land and hunted animals.

2. Complete the chart below.

Main Idea and Details

Group	Where they lived
Modoc	
	Lake Tahoe
Chumash	

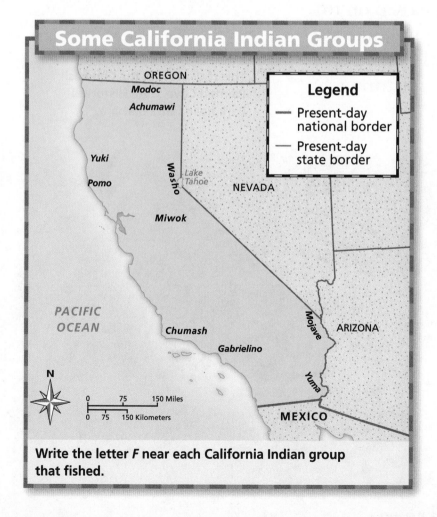

Some California Indian Groups

OREGON

Modoc

Achumawi

Legend
— Present-day national border
— Present-day state border

Yuki

Washo

Lake Tahoe

NEVADA

Pomo

Miwok

PACIFIC OCEAN

Chumash

Mojave

ARIZONA

Gabrielino

Yuma

N

0   75   150 Miles
0   75   150 Kilometers

MEXICO

Write the letter _F_ near each California Indian group that fished.

Passing Down Their History

In the past, most California Indians did not have a written language. Instead, they passed down their history through folklore. **Folklore** is the stories and customs of a group of people. They shared their past through myths and legends. Myths are stories that explain things in nature, and legends are stories about people in the past. California Indians still pass down folklore, myths, and legends today.

California Indians have traditions to celebrate their history. A **tradition** is a special way a group of people does something and that has been passed on to others. For example, some groups, like the Chumash and the Gabrielino, painted or carved pictures on rocks. The pictures often show important events.

3. Compare and Contrast
List two things most California Indian groups of the past had in common.

_____

_____

_____

This rock art is in the Chumash Painted Cave State Historical Park near Santa Barbara.

Beliefs

Many California Indian groups believed in spirits, and some still do. They believed that spirits helped them, but that they also could cause problems for them. Special leaders led the people in ceremonies. A **ceremony** is an important activity done for a special reason. For example, some California Indian leaders might perform a ceremony to get ready for a good hunt.

California Indians Today

Our state is still home to many California Indians. Some of them live on areas of land that their group owns. Some California Indians have moved to cities for jobs. Today, most California Indians dress and live the same way as other Americans. But some California Indians still perform traditional ceremonies. They keep their customs alive for future generations.

Today, about 242,000 American Indians live in California.

4. Why might a leader perform a ceremony?
Cause and Effect

_____

_____

_____

5. Compare and Contrast
In the text, circle the ways in which California Indians today are like the California Indians of the past.

Summary

American Indians had their own customs and traditions before Europeans arrived. Some are still followed today. What are some customs and traditions of California Indians?

Charts

Learn More A chart makes it easier to compare and contrast information. The chart below tells you about four different California Indian groups. A heading at the top of each column tells what information is listed in that column. The heading of the first column is *Group.* This column lists the names of different groups. The information about each group is listed in the other columns. To find information for one group, find that group's name in the first column. Then move your finger to the right to find information about that group in the other columns. Use the chart to answer the questions below.

Try It

1. Underline the region in which the Chumash live. *Identify*

2. Circle the heading you would look under if you wanted to find out if any groups built houses underground. *Identify*

3. How were the foods of the Washo and the Miwok different? *Interpret*

_____

_____

_____

California Indian Life

Group	Region	Foods	Houses
Chumash	Coast	Fish, birds, sea animals	Large, dome-shaped
Miwok	Valley	Acorns, deer	Cone-shaped, partly underground
Washo	Mountain	Deer, antelope	Made from deer, antelope
Yuma	Desert	Seeds, fruit, fish, corn, beans	Square-shaped, sand-covered

Living Traditions

Many different groups of California Indians live in our state. Music, art, and storytelling have been part of their beliefs, customs, and traditions.

Groups

This map shows you where many California Indian groups lived in the different regions of our state.

Find the large red letters on the map. Then look at the letters in the lists below to see which group lived in each region. Many of these groups still live here today.

A. Achumawi
B. Cahuilla
C. Chumash
D. Costanoan
E. Hupa
F. Luiseño
G. Maidu

H. Miwok
I. Mojave
J. Pomo
K. Shasta
L. Yokuts
M. Yuma
N. Yurok

Map Legend

= Coast
= Desert
= Mountain
= Valley

Circle the name of a California Indian group in or near your region.

Art and Music

Coast

Works of Art

The baskets of the Pomo are important to their culture. The Pomo still teach the art of making baskets. It may take several months to make one basket. Some basket makers add feathers from birds such as woodpeckers, blue jays, and ducks. The Pomo may also add beads made from clamshells. Some Pomo baskets are as small as the tip of a finger.

Pomo basket

Valley

Making Music in the Valley

Music was important to many valley Indians. The Miwok made flutes and whistles from the bones of birds. They also split one end of a piece of wood to make a clapper. When someone shook the clapper, it would make a sound.

Bird bones were made into instruments

Mountain

Wood and Bones

Mountain Indians used many resources to make their musical instruments and jewelry. The Hupa carved whistles from wood or animal bones. Rattles were made from deer hooves that were joined to wooden handles. The Maidu used animal bones to make jewelry. Sometimes they added shells and feathers to their necklaces and earrings.

Hupa whistle

Desert

Clay Dolls

Many desert Indians made pottery. Pottery includes pots and dishes made from clay. First, the desert Indians shaped wet clay into pots, dishes, or storage containers. Then they used heat from a fire to dry the clay. The Mojave also used clay to make dolls for their children. They decorated the dolls to look like people. The dolls even had human hair.

Mojave clay doll

Draw a circle around two resources in the text that California Indians used to make whistles.

Beliefs and Customs

Pomo cocoon rattle

Coast

Cocoon Rattles

Special leaders, or what some people called shamans, for the Pomo used healing rattles. The rattles were made from cocoons. Cocoons are the outside covers caterpillars make around themselves. The cocoons were then attached to a wooden handle. Special leaders could then wave the rattle over the sick person.

Valley

Bear Power

Animals and their spirits were important to some valley Indians. Many Yokuts honored animals that were connected with their

Grizzly bear

family group. Some Yokuts had special leaders called bear doctors. They believed these leaders received their power from bears and could even turn into bears.

Hupa Jumping Dance

Mountain

Healers and Dancers

The special leaders of the Hupa performed two important dances. One was the White Deerskin Dance. The other was the Jumping Dance. The Hupa believed these dances kept their people well. They also believed that the dances would bring success in a hunt for animals or fish.

Desert

Bird Singing

Bird songs are an important Cahuilla tradition. These songs tell their history. Bird songs were a part of many ceremonies. Often these songs

took several days to perform. Bird songs are still part of ceremonies today. Bird singing connects the Cahuillas to their past.

> Underline two things in the text that a special leader did.

Folklore

Storytelling is still a part of the lives of many California Indians. Older people in each group pass down their history and traditions to younger people by telling stories.

American Indian storyteller

Coast

Stories of Coyote

Many California Indians tell stories about Coyote. This story comes from the Pomo.

Long ago, the world was dark. So Coyote gathered some grass and made it into a tight ball. Then he asked Hawk to fly into the sky with the ball and light it on fire. This ball became the sun. But there were times when it was dark because North Wind blew the sun across the sky. So Coyote sent Hawk up into the sky with another ball of grass. But this grass was wet. It did not burn as brightly as the first ball. This ball became the moon. When the moon is full, the grandchildren of Coyote remember the wet grass and howl, "The moon is too dim."

Mountain

How Mount Shasta Came to Be

Some mountain Indians tell a story about how Mount Shasta came to be. Years ago, steam and ash would sometimes blow out of an opening in the mountain.

The Old Man Above lived on the other side of the sky. One day he decided to visit Earth. So he threw down ice and snow until he had made a large pile reaching almost to the sky. Then he began his trip to Earth by stepping from cloud to cloud. Soon he reached the pile and scooped out a large hole in it. He moved inside and made his house in that hole. When the Shasta saw steam and smoke rising from the top of the pile, they would say, "Old Man Above is in his house."

Mount Shasta

Circle the two things in the story that came from balls of grass.

Folklore

Valley

Inchworm

A Very Small Hero

The Miwok tell a story about a mountain in Yosemite Valley. Today, that mountain is called El Capitan.

. . . .

Two young brother bears fell asleep on a rock. As they slept, the rock grew and became a mountain. Mother Bear worried because she could not find her bear cubs. Finally, the animals saw the brothers at the top of the mountain. Many big and strong animals tried to leap or climb to the top of the mountain. But none could help. Finally, a tiny inchworm crawled all the way to the top. He took a very long time. But the inchworm showed the brother bears how to get down safely.

Bear cubs

Desert

Colorado River

Great Tellings

The Mojave tell of the First Times, a period of time long ago. They share these stories with their group and call them Great Tellings.

. . . .

Only people lived during the First Times. There were no animals or crops to eat. So the spirit Mastamho stuck a willow stick in the ground. When he pulled out the stick, water flowed onto the land. This water became the Colorado River. It was filled with ducks and fish. Then Mastamho taught the Mojave how to plant seeds to grow crops. He also showed them how to make fire. Later, he taught them how to make pots to use for cooking.

A duck

Underline two things in the story that Mastamho taught the Mojave.

What Is the Culture of the California Indians?

Write the name of the region where you live in the center circle. In the other circles, write one detail that tells about the culture of a group in your region.

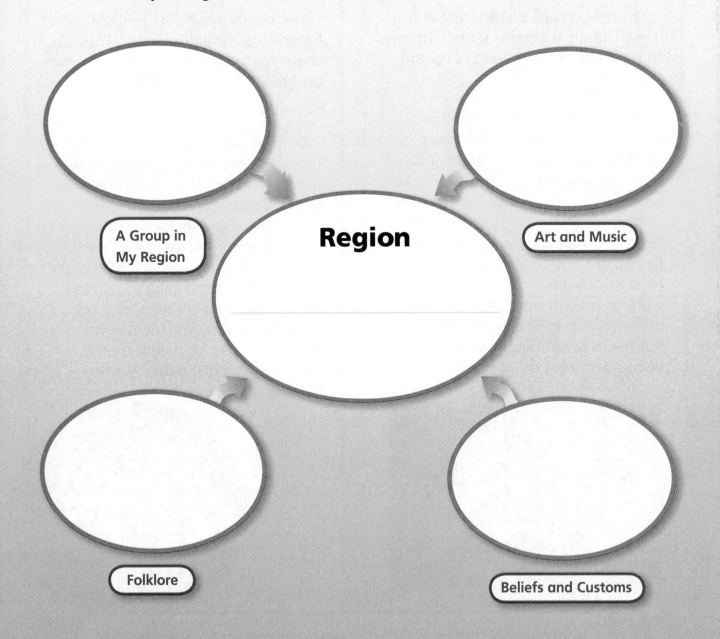

A Group in
My Region

Region

Art and Music

Folklore

Beliefs and Customs

H-SS 3.2.2 Discuss the ways in which physical geography, including climate, influenced how the local Indian nations adapted to their natural environment (e.g., how they obtained food, clothing, tools).

How have California Indians lived in their environment?

CONNECT TO YOU How does where you live affect how you live? California Indians ate food they found in the areas where they lived. They built homes from wood, grasses, and other plants that grew around them.

Preview the Lesson

Vocabulary

weather *(n.)* the temperature and conditions of the air outside at a certain place and time

adapt *(v.)* to change to fit new conditions

climate *(n.)* the weather an area usually has year after year

Vocabulary Activity

Write a sentence below using a vocabulary word from the list above that describes the climate of your region.

_____

_____

Reading: Cause and Effect

A *cause* is why something happens. An *effect* is what happens as a result of the cause. As you read, underline parts of the text that tell why the Achumawi were called Pit River Indians.

▷

Different Environments

California has mountains, valleys, deserts, and a long coastline. These different areas usually have different environments. This means they have different plants, animals, landforms, and weather. **Weather** is the temperature and conditions of the air outside at a certain place and time. California Indians had to adapt to their environment. To **adapt** is to change to fit new conditions.

Food

California Indians ate the food that they could find around them. The Achumawi (ah chu MAH we) lived in the mountain region. They ate acorns and deer, which were found in the mountains. They were called the Pit River Indians because they used pits, or holes in the ground, to trap deer they were hunting. The Pomo lived in the coast region. They gathered food such as seeds, acorns, and berries.

1. Fill in the effect box below.

Cause and Effect

Cause:

Land areas in California have different environments.

Effect:

2. What kinds of food did the Pomo eat? Explain why.

Main Idea and Details

This Achumawi man is making a basket.

Homes

California Indians also adapted how they lived based on their climate. **Climate** is the weather an area usually has year after year. The Modoc lived in the mountain region. They lived in warm homes because winters in the mountains are cold and snowy. The Miwok in the valley region lived in houses made of branches, bark, small bushes, or grass. The Yuma in the desert region made houses from branches and small bushes. They covered their homes with soil or sand to stay cool in the hot sun.

The Hupa in the mountain region made houses out of cedar wood.

Clothing and Tools

California Indians used plants and animal skins to make clothing. Often groups traded with other groups for things that they wanted or needed. The Washo, who lived in the mountain region, hunted deer. They used deer skins to make shirts and pants. They used deer antlers as tools for digging and cutting. The Chumash lived in the coast region. Chumash women wore skirts made from sea grass they found along the coast. California Indians who lived in the desert, such as the Mojave and Yuma, dressed in light clothing to stay cool.

3. How did climate affect the homes the Yuma built?

Cause and Effect

4. Circle the sentences that describe clothes that California Indians made from things in their region.

Main Idea and Details

Summary

California Indians were able to live in many kinds of environments. How did climate affect how they lived?

Climate Maps

Learn More A climate map uses different colors to show the climate areas of regions. The climate map below shows the different climate areas in California. The map legend explains what climate each color on the map stands for. For example, the color green stands for a climate that has a mild, wet winter and a hot, dry summer. Use the map to answer the questions below.

Try It

1. How many different climate areas does this map show? *Identify*

   _____

2. What is the climate area of Sacramento? *Interpret*

   _____

   _____

3. Circle the words on the map legend that describe the climate area of Eureka. *Identify*

4. Which color represents your climate area? *Apply*

   _____

California's Climate Areas

Legend
- Partly dry, temperature varies with north-south location
- Dry, temperature varies with north-south location
- Mild winter, cool summer, wet
- Mild, wet winter; hot, dry summer
- Highlands; temperature and rainfall vary with elevation
— National border
— State border
★ State capital
• Other city

Living on the Land

California Indians used plants, animals, and other natural resources in their region to make what they needed to live.

Environments

Each California region has a different environment and climate.

Draw a circle around the name of the region where you live.

Coast

Mountain

Valley

Desert

Houses

Coast

Homes Made of Plants and Wood

The coast Indians built their homes from plants and trees in their region. The Yurok made their homes out of wood from redwood trees. The Pomo started their homes by putting up a frame of wooden poles. Then they covered the poles with oak or willow tree branches. Finally, they covered their homes with tule grass.

Tule is a kind of tall grass that grows in water.

Pomo house

Mountain

Homes Built Underground

The Hupa dug deep into the ground to make their houses. Then they made shelves of packed dirt next to the underground walls. The ceiling and upper walls were made of boards from cedar trees in the region. Each home had a fire pit in the middle for cooking and to heat the home.

Hupa cedar house

What did mountain and coast Indians use to build their homes?

_____

_____

Valley

Homes Made of Grass

The Yokuts and Miwok built cone-shaped houses. First, they dug a shallow ditch and made a frame out of poles. Then they wove tree branches through the frame. Next, they tied bunches of dried grass to the branches. Finally, they made the roof out of bark from cedar or pine trees.

Miwok house

Desert

Summer Home, Winter Home

What kind of house would you build if you lived where it is hot and dry? Some desert Indians had houses made of bushes and wood. They built part of their houses underground for protection from the hot sun. In winter the Mojave piled mud over their homes to keep warm.

Mojave Desert

In the text, circle one resource used in the valley and one resource used in the desert to build houses.

Foods

Coast

Foods from the Sea

Foods: fish, shellfish, sea birds, seaweed, antelope, seals, whales, grapes, honey

Coast Indians got most of their food from the ocean. They stood in the water and used a big net to catch fish. They gathered clams, mussels, and crabs, and caught sea birds in large nets.

Mountain

Baked Grasshoppers

Foods: grapes, elk, raccoons, squirrels, quail, ducks, grasshoppers, seeds

Have you ever caught a grasshopper? The Maidu caught grasshoppers to eat them. First, the Maidu used tree branches to move grasshoppers into holes filled with water. Then they used baskets to scoop the grasshoppers out of the holes. Finally, they baked them before eating.

> Circle the names of two regions where California Indians ate grasshoppers.

Valley

Eating Acorns

Foods: acorns, shellfish, plants, roots, grasshoppers, elk, birds, antelope

Many valley Indians ate acorns. How did they eat them? First, they put acorns into a hole in a rock and ground them. Then they soaked the ground acorns to make them taste good. Finally, they cooked them to make a thick soup.

Holes for grinding acorns

Ground acorns

> Many California Indians ate acorns, seeds, deer, fish, nuts, berries, bears, and rabbits. What other foods did they eat in each region?

Desert

Prickly pear cactus

Cactus Snacks

Foods: corn, gourds, beans, pumpkins, cactus, bighorn sheep, insects

Cactus was one important food for many desert Indians. They ate the fruit of the prickly pear cactus. Sometimes they dried the fruit in the sun to make it stay fresh longer.

Clothing

Coast

Feathers and Fur

In winter the coast Indians wore clothes made from feathers and animal skins. First, they dried skins from deer, rabbits, or sea otters. Then they shaped the skins into robes and blankets. The Luiseño also made shoes out of animal skins.

Deerskin

Valley

Clothes of Grass and Skin

Most valley Indians made their clothing from plants and animal skins. Yokut women made cloth from tule and willow tree bark. In winter men and women wore robes and dresses made of animal skins.

Miwok chief

Mountain

Getting Dressed with Shells

Mountain Indians often used shells to make their clothes. Many Hupa women wore skirts woven from bear grass and shells. They also strung pine nut shells on bear grass to make aprons. They decorated aprons and skirts with pieces of clamshells or other shells for special ceremonies. The Hupa decorated headdresses with feathers from birds, such as owls and woodpeckers.

Hupa woman

> In the text, circle the kinds of resources that California Indians used to make clothes.

Desert

Robes in the Desert

Many desert Indian women wore aprons made of tree bark. Desert Indians often wore sandals made of woven fibers from yucca plants. The sandals protected their feet when they walked over rough ground. Even in the hot desert the weather was cold in winter. Many desert Indians wore robes made of rabbit skin to stay warm.

Jack rabbit

Tools

Yurok elk horn purse

Coast

Many Kinds of Tools

The coast Indians used many resources from their region to make tools. Thin fibers from plants such as milkweed were made into rope. The Chumash carved plates and bowls out of wood. The Yurok made purses out of elk horns and seashells.

Many California Indians were skilled at making baskets. The baskets were made from different parts of plants. They had many uses.

Timbisha basket

Valley

Fishing and Hunting Tools

Obsidian spear point

Valley Indians used wood, rocks, and plants for their fishing and hunting tools. The Miwok carved fishing spears from wood. Spear points were made from a hard, glassy rock called obsidian. Valley Indians made fishing nets out of plant fibers.

Mojave man with bow and arrows

Mountain

Fishing on the River

Hupa weir on the Trinity River

The mountain Indians used different tools to fish. The Hupa fished with nets. When the river was low in summer, they built a weir, a large wooden dam, across it. Then they sat on top of the dam and dipped large nets into the water to catch fish.

Desert

Tools Made of Plants and Clay

The desert Indians used several resources to make tools. Some made baskets from reeds and grass. The Mojave made pots from clay. They shaped wood into bows and arrows.

Underline six tools and other useful things in the text that California Indians made from wood.

Ways of Travel

Coast Indians row a balsa in San Francisco Bay.

Coast

Traveling by Canoes

Coast Indians used balsas and canoes to travel on the water. Balsas were bundles of tule tied together. The Chumash built boats out of cedar. The Yuroks made canoes by digging out the inside of tree trunks.

Mountain

Redwood Canoes

Canoes were an important way to travel for many mountain Indians. The Hupa made their canoes from redwood logs. They used the canoes on the Trinity River.

Redwood trees

Valley

Other Ways of Travel

The valley Indians did not use canoes. Many of them swam. Those who could not swim traveled on logs pushed along by swimmers. Some valley Indians also used balsas to carry people and supplies on rivers.

Desert

Drifting and Floating

The Yuma and Mojave lived near rivers but did not make canoes. They often drifted along rivers on rafts. Sometimes they floated supplies in hollow logs. Many desert Indians swam next to large bowls of clothing and bedding they floated on rivers.

In the text, circle the different ways California Indians traveled on water.

How Did California Indians Live?

Complete the sentence in the center box below by writing in the region in which you live. Then list facts about the California Indians in your region in each box.

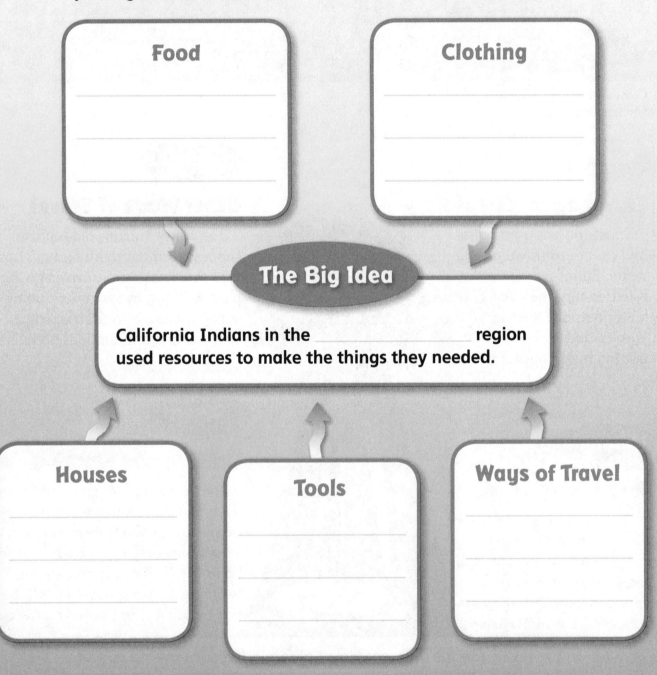

Food

Clothing

The Big Idea

California Indians in the _____ region used resources to make the things they needed.

Houses

Tools

Ways of Travel

H-SS 3.2.3 Describe the economy and systems of government, particularly those with tribal constitutions, and their relationship to federal and state governments.

How do California Indian groups function?

CONNECT TO YOU Do you have rules at home? Many American Indian groups have a written plan that explains the rules for their members.

Preview the Lesson

Vocabulary

reservation *(n.)* an area of land owned by an American Indian group

government *(n.)* the people who run a state or country, or the laws of a state or country

laws *(n.)* rules made by a government

constitution *(n.)* a written plan for a government

economy *(n.)* the way things are made and are bought and sold in a country, region, state, or local area

Vocabulary Activity Choose the vocabulary words above that best complete the sentence below.

The _____ of a country

are made by people who run the

_____ .

Reading: Compare and Contrast

Remember that to *compare* means to describe how two or more things are alike. To *contrast* means to describe how they are different. Underline the sentence on page 42 that compares or contrasts two things.

American Indian Land

Today, some American Indians live on reservations or on smaller reservations called rancherias. A **reservation** is an area of land owned by an American Indian group.

How Tribal Governments Work

American Indian reservations have tribal governments. A **government** is the people who run a state or country, or the laws of a state or country. **Laws** are rules made by a government. Tribal governments are separate from the government of our state and are overseen by the U.S. government. Two kinds of American Indian governments are tribal councils and general councils. They make laws for the reservation. Like our cities and states, some councils provide police forces, which make sure laws are followed, and firefighting services. Some reservations also have their own courts and judges.

This California Indian police officer works on a reservation near Indio.

1. ⟳ Compare and Contrast

How are reservations and rancherias different?

2. **What function do tribal and general councils have?**

Main Idea and Details

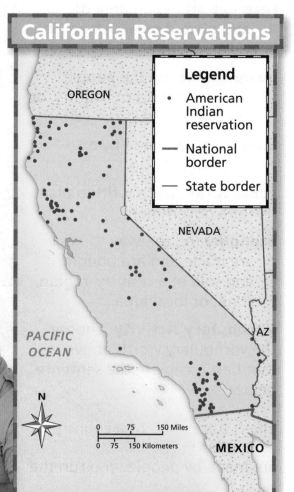

California Reservations

Legend
- • American Indian reservation
- ▬ National border
- — State border

OREGON

NEVADA

PACIFIC OCEAN

AZ

N

0   75   150 Miles

0   75   150 Kilometers

MEXICO

There are about 100 reservations in our state. Circle the symbol for a reservation on the map legend.

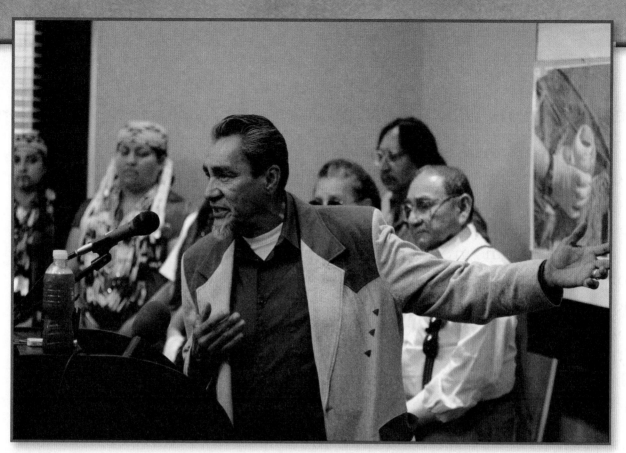

A California Indian tribal council member speaks about the condition of the Klamath River in northern California.

Some American Indian tribal governments make laws much like our state government does. These laws make sure that people are kept safe. They also make sure that people have a right to vote and to own land.

Written Plans for Government

Many tribal governments, such as the Cahuilla, have their own constitutions. A **constitution** is a written plan for a government. These constitutions have a preamble, just like the U.S. and California Constitutions. A preamble is an introduction. These constitutions also have parts, called articles, that give more details about the laws.

3. ⊙ Compare and Contrast

How is the Cahuilla constitution like the U.S. Constitution?

_____

_____

_____

Reservations Make Money

California Indians help our state's economy in many ways. An **economy** is the way that things are made and are bought and sold in a country, region, state, or local area. Some groups run farms or stores. Many groups welcome visitors to their reservations and rancherias. These visitors may spend money on camping or arts and crafts, such as baskets and jewelry. They may come to enjoy entertainment, such as dancing, singing, and storytelling.

Some groups, such as the Yuroks, fish. They keep some of their catch for themselves and sell the rest to people outside the reservation.

4. Name three things visitors to a reservation or rancheria might buy.
Main Idea and Details

This Hupa man is caring for young trees in a greenhouse.

This Pomo woman is weaving a basket.

Helping the Economy

The money that people spend on reservations and rancherias helps our economy. California Indians can then spend this money outside the reservation or rancheria. They buy things they need and want and pay for activities, such as banking, in nearby towns. The businesses in the towns also pay money to our state government and the U.S. government. The government uses the money to build or improve schools, roads, and parks, among other things.

5. Describe the flow of money out of a reservation or rancheria. *Sequence*

_____

_____

_____

_____

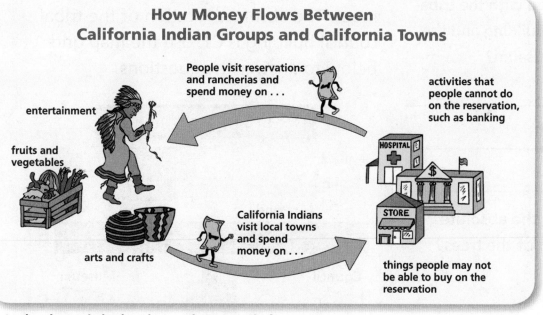

How Money Flows Between California Indian Groups and California Towns

People visit reservations and rancherias and spend money on . . .

activities that people cannot do on the reservation, such as banking

entertainment

fruits and vegetables

HOSPITAL

STORE

arts and crafts

California Indians visit local towns and spend money on . . .

things people may not be able to buy on the reservation

In the chart, circle the places where people from the reservation spend money.

Summary

Tribal governments use constitutions to set up rules for reservations. How are tribal governments like state and national governments?

Relative Location and Absolute Location

Learn More You can describe where most places are by using relative or absolute location. Relative location tells you where something is by comparing it with the location of another place. To describe the tribal council building's relative location on the map grid below, you could say that it is close to the parking lot.

Absolute location tells you more exactly where something is. You can use a map grid to find both relative and absolute location. Each square has both a letter and a number based on where the letter column and number column meet. The absolute location of the tribal council building is C1. Use the map grid below to answer the questions.

Try It

1. Circle the place with an absolute location of A1. *Identify*

2. What is the relative location of the parking lot compared with the tribal council building and the tribal museum? *Interpret*

_____

_____

_____

3. What is the absolute location of the trees? *Identify*

_____

4. Draw a house in the relative location between the pond and the farm. *Apply*

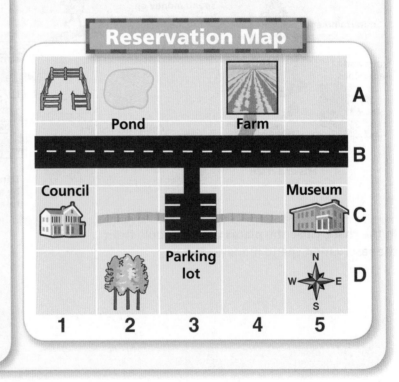

Reservation Map

Planning and Working

California Indians have combined their way of life with new ways of governing themselves and doing business.

California Indian Nations

Did you know that many California Indians are members of a California Indian group, our state, and our country?

Some California Indians are members of a California Indian nation. The U.S. government made agreements with American Indian groups in the same way that it did with other nations. More than 100 of these nations are in California.

The United States

Mountain
Hoopa Valley Tribe (Hupa)

Valley
Tuolumne Band of Me-Wuk (Miwok) Indians

Coast
Santa Ynez Band of Chumash Indians

Desert
Agua Caliente Band of Cahuilla Indians

California

Underline the California Indian nation in your region.

Coast

From a Leader to a Business Committee

Many years ago, each Chumash village had a leader called a wot. The wot could be a man or a woman. The wot would make important decisions for the group.

Today, many Chumash live on the Santa Ynez Reservation. They have their own constitution. These Chumash elect, or choose, five people to a business committee. This committee decides important matters for the Chumash. All Chumash adults have a voice in decisions that the committee makes.

A Chumash from today in traditional clothing

Valley

Meeting in the Roundhouse

In the past, most Miwok groups had a leader. The leader would assign jobs during the acorn harvest, solve problems, greet guests, and take care of ceremonies. Sometimes the leader would meet with people in the roundhouse.

Today, many Miwok live on rancherias. Each group has a constitution. Most rancherias elect a tribal council. The council works to improve things like schools and health care. Sometimes the Tuolumne Rancheria council still meets in the roundhouse.

Circle the names of the small groups elected by some Chumash and Miwok.

Outside and inside a Miwok council roundhouse

Mountain

Working Together

A long time ago, the Hupa lived in seven villages in the Hoopa Valley. Each village had its own leader. The people of the villages worked together as a group. They would meet for special ceremonies. They would also join together to protect themselves.

Today, the Hupa run all parts of their government. They have had a constitution for more than fifty years. The Hupa elect a tribal council. They operate their own hospital, police and fire departments, and schools.

A view of the Hoopa Valley Indian Reservation

Put a checkmark next to the regions that have groups with constitutions.

Desert

Cahuilla Leaders

In the Cahuilla groups there was a person called a nét. He made sure that songs and ceremonies were performed correctly. He also made important decisions for the group.

Today, there are nine Cahuilla groups called bands. Each band elects its own tribal council. A tribal council makes the rules for a band. The Agua Caliente band has a constitution that explains the duties of its tribal council. One of those duties is to protect the natural resources on the group's land.

Protecting natural resources like Palm Canyon is one duty of the Cahuilla tribal councils.

Economy

Coast

New Uses for the Land

The Luiseño have found new uses for the land where they fished, hunted, and gathered food long ago. One group of the Luiseño runs a campground on its reservation near San Diego. The San Luis Rey River, which cuts through the reservation, is used for tubing, swimming, and fishing. Visitors come to the reservations for these activities.

Another group of Luiseño planted orchards on its reservation. The group grows and sells oranges, lemons, and avocados. These activities help the economy.

avocados

orange

lemon

Valley

Big Time

The Miwok celebrate the Big Time, or acorn festival, each fall. The Big Time allows the Miwok to teach other people about their traditions. It also helps them earn money from the visitors who come to see the festival. Many visitors come to the Acorn Festival at the Tuolumne Rancheria. They enjoy watching the dancers, buying arts and crafts, eating food, and playing games.

A traditional Miwok dance

Write two ways that visitors help the economy of the Luiseño or the Miwok.

_____

_____

Mountain

Fish Tag

The Hupa have always fished as part of their way of life. Today, the Hupa run a fish hatchery with the government of California. A hatchery is a place that protects young fish after they hatch from eggs. Later, the fish are let go into streams and rivers. The Hupa put little tags on the young fish to track them after they are let go. When the fish grow larger, they can be caught and sold. This work helps the region's economy.

A Hupa fisheries employee shows his salmon catch from the Trinity River

> Underline one sentence in each paragraph that explains how the Hupa and Agua Caliente help the economy in their region.

Desert

Canyon Sights

The hot springs of Palm Springs have played an important part in the history of the Agua Caliente, a Cahuilla group. The springs provided water for the group. Later, the springs became a way for them to earn money. The Cahuilla run a resort near the hot springs. Visitors come to stay at the resort or tour the canyons nearby. The Cahuilla continue to protect the canyons where they hunted and gathered food a long time ago.

Visitors ride horses through the canyons on the Agua Caliente's land.

What is important about the economy and government of the California Indians in my region?

Coast   **Valley**   **Mountain**   **Desert**

Circle the picture above from your region. Write a sentence below about the picture that tells about the economy of the California Indians in your region.

List two facts about the government today of the California Indians in your region.

1.

2.

How did Europeans change life for California Indians?

SET THE SCENE What would you do if you were moving into a new house, but someone already lived there? That is what happened when Europeans came to North America. The land they wanted to live on was already home to many American Indian groups.

Preview the Lesson
Vocabulary

interact *(v.)* to talk to other people and work with them

settler *(n.)* someone who goes to live in a new place

cooperate *(v.)* to work together

conflict *(n.)* a struggle or disagreement

mission *(n.)* a settlement set up by a religious group to teach religion and other ways of life to native people

religion *(n.)* a system of faith and worship

Vocabulary Activity Draw a line to connect the two vocabulary words above that have almost the same meaning.

Reading: Cause and Effect

Remember that a *cause* is why something happens. An *effect* is what happens as a result of the cause. Underline the sentence on page 54 that tells the effect on California Indians of diseases brought over by Spanish settlers.

▶

1767 Spain sends Gaspar de Portolá to run its land in California.

1775 A few California Indians destroy a mission.

The Spanish Arrive

The Spanish came to what is now California in the 1700s. Many were looking for land and riches. About 300,000 California Indians lived in the region at that time. The Spanish interacted with them. To **interact** means to talk to other people and work with them. In 1767 Spain sent Gaspar de Portolá to run its land in California.

The arrival of these settlers changed the lives of many California Indians. A **settler** is someone who goes to live in a new place. Some Spanish settlers wanted California Indians to build and work on missions. **Missions** are settlements set up by religious groups to teach religion and other ways of life to native people. **Religion** is a system of faith and worship.

Many California Indians had lived by hunting and gathering before the Spanish came. But some settlers made some of them farm and look after the animals. Many of them also had to speak Spanish instead of their own languages. Some got sick from diseases that the settlers had brought over with them from Spain. This caused the California Indian population to go down.

1. Write one effect for the cause below.

Cause and Effect

Cause		Effect
The Spanish settled in present-day California.	→	

1800s

Some Spanish settlers made many California Indians work on farms at the missions.

Trying to Get Along

Sometimes the Spanish settlers got along with the California Indians. At other times, they did not get along. One way they got along was through trade. They **cooperated,** or worked together, when they traded.

Spanish settlers wanted more land during the 1800s. One reason why the settlers needed land was for their animals. This was land that the California Indians had been living on for a long time. The need for land soon led to conflicts between the settlers and the California Indians. A **conflict** is a struggle or disagreement. In 1775 a few California Indians fought back by destroying a mission in San Diego.

2. Compare and Contrast

Underline one way California Indians and Spanish settlers got along and one way they did not.

Summary

When Europeans arrived, life changed for many of the California Indians. How did the two groups interact?

Diaries: Father Pedro Font

Learn More A primary source is a description of an event by someone who was there when the event happened. Primary sources can be diaries, letters, documents, interviews, and even paintings and photographs. The primary source below is from the diary of Father Pedro Font. Diaries can tell us about the thoughts and feelings of people who lived long ago.

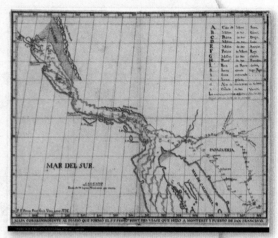

Father Font traveled to California with Spanish settlers in the late 1700s. He wrote in his diary about meeting American Indians from many different groups. Below, read Father Font's diary entry. Then answer the questions.

1. **Underline the things that the Cajuenche Indians brought to trade with the Spanish.** Identify

2. **Why did Father Font and the other settlers stay at the lake?** Analyze

_____

_____

_____

_____

In order that the horses and mules, which were in bad condition, might be refreshed with the good grass around this pond, it was determined that we should remain here. Many Indians of the Cajuenche nation, who live from here on farther down the river, came joyfully, and brought to the camp a great many watermelons, pumpkins, and other provisions [food supplies], which they traded for beads.

—_December 7, 1775_

Interacting with Others

The California Indians interacted with settlers and others who came to their area. Some of the meetings were friendly. Others were not.

Gift Giving and Trade

The California Indians and the settlers cooperated by giving gifts to or trading with one another.

The California Indians sometimes offered food, such as nuts, fruits, vegetables, or fish, to the settlers after their long trips. They were happy to receive metal tools from the settlers. The California Indians were also interested in cloth and European clothing. Some California Indians traded beaver fur with the settlers.

Fish

Watermelons and Pumpkins

Draw a circle around one thing the California Indians might have given to the settlers. Draw an arrow next to one thing the settlers might have given in return.

Beaver Fur

Metal Tools

Cloth

Acorns

Berries

Something's Fishy

Did you know that fish were probably one of the first gifts given by California Indians to Europeans? Juan Rodríguez Cabrillo's ships were sailing along the coast in 1542. Some Chumash came out in their canoes to greet Cabrillo and his crew from Spain. The Chumash brought fish for them to eat.

Chumash canoes were called *tomols*.

Mission Chumash

The Spanish returned to California in the 1700s to build settlements. Some Spanish settlers wanted California Indians to become Catholic and live like them. They wanted the Chumash to live and work at the missions. Some Chumash agreed to do this. Others were forced.

California Indians used washbasins to wash their clothes at Mission Santa Barbara.

The Chumash had hunted and fished in this area for hundreds of years. But the Spanish wanted the Chumash to learn new skills. The Spanish taught the Chumash how to farm and to care for animals, such as cows and horses. Some Chumash became cowboys. Others did not want to give up their way of life and escaped from the Spanish.

Many Chumash lived and worked at the Mission Santa Barbara.

Circle two things some Chumash did before the Spanish came to California. Next, underline two new skills some Chumash learned from the Spanish.

Desert

They Led the Way

Who would you ask to lead you across a desert? The Mojave knew the way across the Mojave Desert. They followed footpaths that they had used for many years. In 1776 some Mojave led Father Francisco Garcés, a Spanish priest, and his group across the desert. This helped the Spanish learn how to travel by land from Mexico to their missions in California. In 1826 the Mojave helped guide Jedediah Smith, an American fur trader, along paths through the Mojave Desert.

With help from the Mojave, Jedediah Smith and his group become the first Americans to reach California by land from the east.

A Fight over Fur

Jedediah Smith wrote in his journal that the Mojave treated him with great kindness. He also described the melons and roasted pumpkins they gave him. But problems started when the fur trappers arrived. A trapper is a person who catches animals for their fur. The Mojave thought that the trappers did not show respect for the animals they caught. The trappers used only the fur of the animal and wasted the rest of it.

Trappers and the Mojave

In 1827 the Mojave and some trappers began to fight. The Mojave asked for a horse in exchange for the beavers the trappers were taking from the river. The trappers would not agree to this trade. Then the two sides began to fight. The fighting between the trappers and the Mojave went on and off for about twenty years.

Beavers live along the Colorado River in the desert region. They nearly disappeared because so many were caught by trappers in the 1800s.

Circle the names of the people the Mojave helped across the desert.

Forced to Move

The Yokuts first met the Spanish in 1772. They were friendly to the Spanish. But in the early 1800s, some settlers came back with Spanish soldiers. They needed more people to work at their missions on the coast. The Spanish took many Yokuts to these missions. Many had to change the way they lived.

The Yokuts lived in the San Joaquin Valley. There they hunted and gathered their food.

California Indians made ropes at missions.

A Different Way of Life

Many Yokuts were unhappy at the missions. They had to learn a new religion. They could no longer hunt and fish and gather food. Instead, Spanish priests made them work on farms. Some Yokuts became very good at training horses and raising cattle. They lived in crowded tiny cabins. Hundreds of Yokuts became sick and died. Yet some of them escaped from the missions. They lived in freedom far from the coast.

Underline two things in the text that changed the way of life for the Yokuts.

The Mission Santa Clara de Asis was one of the missions where some Yokuts were brought to work and live.

Hidden Away

The mountains around the Hoopa Valley kept most visitors away from the Hupa who lived there. For many years, no European or American settlers made it as far north as this valley. The Hupa fished in the Trinity River and hunted in the valley's forests. Finally, in 1828 the Hupa met some Americans who were led by Jedediah Smith. Later, they met fur trappers who passed through the mountains.

Sometimes Hupa men fished with a spear.

Gold Changes Everything

In 1848 gold was discovered in California. Soon many miners came to the area where the Hupa lived. The miners were looking for gold, so they cut down many trees and put waste in the rivers. Their actions made it hard for the Hupa to hunt deer and fish.

There's Gold in the Hills!

The discovery of gold brought many settlers onto California Indian lands.

This is one of the first pieces of gold discovered in California.

Circle two things below that were harder for the Hupa to find after the miners came.

Losing Their Lands

More settlers came here after California became a state in 1850. They wanted the land for their own farms, ranches, towns, and businesses. Some settlers attacked California Indian groups. They tried to drive them off land that the groups had lived on for hundreds of years. Some of the groups fought back. By the late 1800s, some California Indians were living on reservations. Many others owned no land at all.

Some Yokuts lived near Tulare Lake in the San Joaquin Valley until the early 1930s.

A California Indian woman shows a child how to weave a basket.

California Indians Today

Today, California Indians live on reservations and in cities and towns around our state. They take pride in their traditions and share them with others. They perform songs and dances. They speak their group's language and teach it to their children. They make crafts in new and old ways. Throughout our state, California Indians continue to celebrate their past as they look to the future.

American Indians' traditional dance at a festival in California

List one way that California Indians take pride in their traditions.

_____

Explore a Museum

To find out more, you can visit a museum in your town or city.

Coast

If you want to learn how to dig carefully for objects from the past, sign up for the "Dig It" program at the Southwest Museum of the American Indian in Los Angeles. You will find out that objects buried underground can tell us much about the California Indians and the settlers they met.

Desert

Have you ever wondered how California Indians made fire without matches? What did they eat? How did they cook it? You can find out the answers and grind corn yourself at the Antelope Valley Indian Museum in the Mojave Desert near Lancaster.

> Circle one thing you would like to see or do at one of the museums. Underline the name of the museum.

Valley

You can try using California Indian tools in the "hands-on" area of the California State Indian Museum in Sacramento. You can also see California Indian houses, hunting tools, musical instruments, and a canoe.

Mountain

Did you know that some of the most beautiful baskets in the world have been made by California Indians? If you go to the Eastern California Museum in Independence, you can see a collection of baskets made by the Paiute and the Shoshone.

What Happened in My Region?

Circle the California Indian group nearest to the region where you live. Next, choose three important events that happened between the settlers and the California Indian group you circled. Finally, put the events in the order in which they happened in the boxes below.

Hupa

Yokuts

Chumash

Mojave

1

2

3

List one way that California Indians celebrate their way of life today.

_____

_____

To find out more, I could visit this museum in my region:

_____

Name:

Study Journal

In this unit you will learn how to put some of California's historical events in the correct sequence. You will see how places changed as different groups of people moved into different areas. Complete the activities on these pages as you read the unit.

What I know about . . .

settlement in California:

People Who Explored or Settled in California

Write in the missing information below.

Three people who explored California were	Workers came to California because	Settlers came to California because

Choose one item below. Tell why it is important to California.

- gold
- computers
- transcontinental railroad
- oranges
- movies

_____

_____

_____

_____

_____

Draw a picture and write about the most interesting person in the unit.

Fill in the missing information on the time line below.

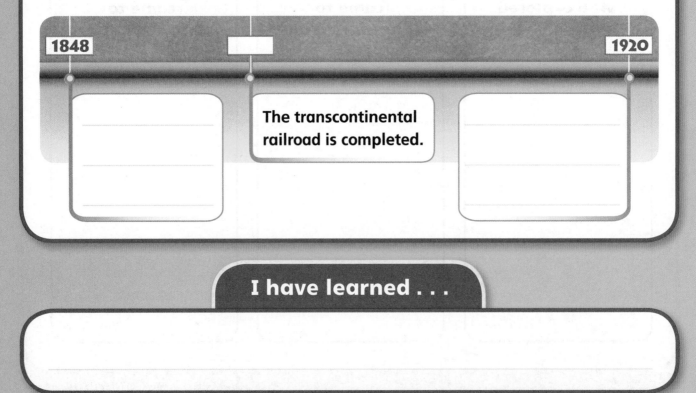

1848		1920
	The transcontinental railroad is completed.	

I have learned . . .

_____

_____

H-SS 3.3.1 Research the explorers who visited here, the newcomers who settled here, and the people who continue to come to the region, including their cultural and religious traditions and contributions.

Who has come to your region?

SET THE SCENE Why have people come to live in your region? Europeans first arrived in present-day California in the 1500s. People from many different places followed. They all came for different reasons. How have they helped make your region what it is today?

Preview the Lesson

Vocabulary

explorer *(n.)* someone who travels to new places to learn more about them

culture *(n.)* the arts, beliefs, behavior, and ideas of a group of people

Vocabulary Activity To *explore* means to travel to new places to learn more about them. Underline the word above that means "one who explores."

People

Juan Rodríguez Cabrillo
Sebastián Vizcaíno
Francis Drake
John Sutter

Reading: Sequence

Writers often include dates to show a *sequence,* or order of events. Circle important dates about explorers who came to California in the first paragraph on page 69. Use the time line at the top of each page to help you keep track of events. ▶

67

Present-day California

1542 Juan Rodríguez Cabrillo explores present-day San Diego Bay.

A European ship from the late 1500s sets sail for a voyage.

In Search of New Lands

European explorers set sail in search of new lands in the 1500s and 1600s. An **explorer** is someone who travels to new places to learn more about them. Sometimes rulers agreed to pay for these trips. Explorers often had to give a share of what they found. Explorers sometimes paid for trips on their own. They hoped to gain wealth through trade and from the land they explored to pay for their trips.

Many European explorers traveled to the Americas. They were looking for land or riches, such as gold and silver. Explorers were also looking for a new trade route between Europe and Asia. One of the reasons that explorers from Spain came to the Americas was to spread the Roman Catholic religion.

1. Name one important way that explorers from Spain were different from other European explorers.

Compare and Contrast

_____

_____

_____

_____

| 1560 | 1580 | 1600 |

1579

1602 Sebastián Vizcaíno explores and names Monterey Bay.

Explorers Reach California

European explorers came to California during the 1500s and 1600s. Three of these explorers were Juan Rodríguez Cabrillo and Sebastián Vizcaíno of Spain and Francis Drake of England. Cabrillo sailed from Mexico to what is now San Diego Bay in 1542. He became one of the first Europeans to see California. Drake landed in a bay north of what is now San Francisco Bay in 1579. It was later named Drake's Bay. Vizcaíno explored and named Monterey Bay in 1602.

Exploring California

- San Francisco
- Monterey
- San Diego

Write a *D* in the place where Drake explored. Write a *V* in the place where Vizcaíno explored. Write a *C* in the place where Cabrillo explored.

2. ⊙ Sequence **Fill in the boxes below to show the sequence of explorations that you read about. Include the name of each explorer.**

First

Next

Last

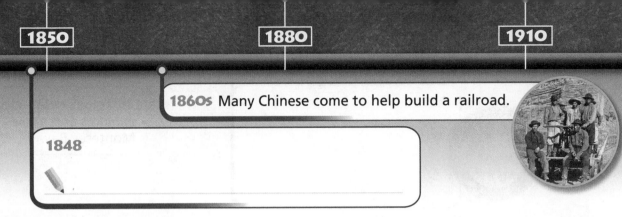
Gold Brings Growth

The number of people living in California grew in the 1840s. John Sutter came to California in 1839. He started a farming settlement. His life changed in 1848. One of Sutter's workers found gold on a piece of his land near present-day Sacramento. News of the discovery spread. Soon thousands of people came to the area from around the world with the hope of getting rich.

Gold was discovered at Sutter's Mill (*far right*) in 1848.

3. What brought many people to California after 1848?

Main Idea and Details

The Railroad Brings Growth

The transcontinental railroad brought even more new people to California. This railroad helped connect the East Coast with the West Coast. It made traveling the long distance easier. Many Chinese workers came here in the 1860s to help build this railroad. Some chose to stay after the railroad was finished to farm or start businesses.

4. In what way did California change because of the transcontinental railroad?

Cause and Effect

2004 California's population is about 35 million.

California's Many People

California's population has grown much since the 1800s. California had about 35 million people in 2004. That is more than any state in the country. People have come here to work in farming, electronics, the military, and other fields.

Large numbers of Hispanics, Asians, Europeans, and other groups have brought the culture of their homelands to California. **Culture** is the arts, beliefs, behavior, and ideas of a group of people. Californians have adopted many parts of these cultures. You can see this in the festivals held across our state.

5. In the text, underline the sentences that tell why we celebrate different festivals in our state. *Cause and Effect*

Danish Americans in Solvang celebrate the Danish Days festival.

Mexican Americans in Los Angeles celebrate Cinco de Mayo.

Japanese Americans in San Francisco celebrate the Cherry Blossom Festival.

Summary

Many groups of people have come to California for different reasons. Compare and contrast the reasons that the first Europeans came to California with those of people who are coming today.

Time Lines

Learn More A time line helps you keep track of events It shows the dates on which events took place. Use these steps to read a time line:

1. Study the title to learn what the time line is about.
2. Figure out the time period the time line covers.
3. Read the time line from left to right. The event on the far left is the oldest event. The event on the far right is the most recent event.

The time lines below compare California events with events that happened in the United States during the same time period. Study the time lines and then answer the questions.

Try It

1. **What time period do the two time lines cover?** *Identify*

   _____

2. **Underline the event that is the earliest.** *Interpret*

3. **Circle the year that California became the thirty-first state.** *Identify*

4. **What California event happened two years after the United States went to war with Mexico?** *Apply*

   _____

   _____

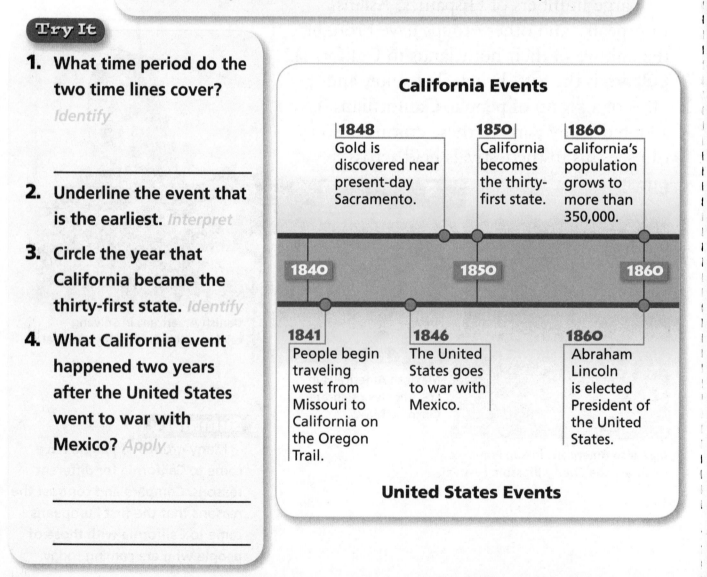

California Events

1848 Gold is discovered near present-day Sacramento.

1850 California becomes the thirty-first state.

1860 California's population grows to more than 350,000.

1840   1850   1860

1841 People begin traveling west from Missouri to California on the Oregon Trail.

1846 The United States goes to war with Mexico.

1860 Abraham Lincoln is elected President of the United States.

United States Events

H-SS 3.3.2 Describe the economies established by settlers and their influence on the present-day economy, with emphasis on the importance of private property and entrepreneurship.

How did early settlers affect your region's economy?

SET THE SCENE When you bite into a sweet, juicy California orange, do you think of gold? Probably not. But the rush to find gold helped California farming. How did gold miners and other settlers help shape California's economy?

Preview the Lesson

Vocabulary

ownership (n.) having something that belongs only to you

property (n.) a thing someone owns

laborer (n.) a worker

good (n.) a thing that is made or grown and then sold

service (n.) a job that someone does for others and for which he or she is usually paid

Vocabulary Activity Use a word from the list above that best completes the sentence:

_____ is something that someone owns, such as a bicycle.

People

James Marshall   Levi Strauss

Reading: Cause and Effect

Remember that a *cause* is why something happens. An *effect* is what happens as a result of the cause. Underline the word *so*, which shows an effect, when you read page 74.

▶

1754 Rancho grants are first given out in California.

Rancho Grants

Beginning in 1754, Spanish and Mexican officials granted, or gave, land called ranchos to people to encourage them to farm and start businesses. These people got full **ownership,** which means having something that belongs only to them. So it became their private **property,** or a thing they own.

Early Businesses and Trade

Many people came to California in the 1800s to start new businesses. In 1804 Father Antonio Cruzado from Spain planted what became California's first orange grove. Today, California leads the country in the growing of fruits.

James Marshall, a **laborer,** or worker, found gold while he was working at a sawmill near present-day Sacramento in 1848. Soon, about 100,000 people came to California looking for gold during the Gold Rush. Many of these people did not find gold but stayed and worked as laborers or set up businesses.

Levi Strauss moved to San Francisco in 1853 after the Gold Rush. Later, he and another man saw that miners needed strong pants. So they started to make and sell denim blue jeans in 1873.

1. How do you think the people felt about owning the ranchos? *Predict*

_____

_____

_____

2. Fill in the effect for the cause below.

Cause and Effect

Cause		Effect
Miners needed stronger pants.	→	

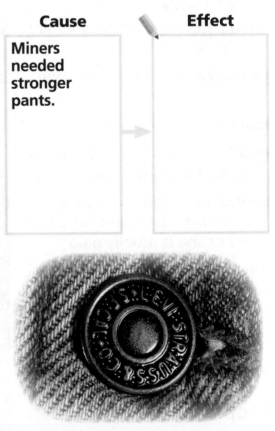

Levi Strauss's company still makes blue jeans today.

1804

1848 James Marshall finds gold near present-day Sacramento.

1853 Levi Strauss moves to San Francisco.

Businesses Continue to Grow

Over time, California has needed laborers to help its economy grow. These workers have made goods and provided services. **Goods** are things that are made or grown and then sold. A **service** is a job that someone does for others and for which he or she is usually paid. People came here in the 1930s to look for work. Many worked on farms. Today, our state is one of the top growers of fruits and vegetables. The Los Angeles area became the center of the movie-making business by 1920. It still is today. People have come to the San Francisco Bay area since the 1960s to start businesses that make computer parts.

3. How did laborers help California grow?

Main Idea and Details

Silicon Valley in Northern California is home to many computer businesses.

Summary

Many settlers helped the economy of California become what it is today. Name one business that still exists today in California that was started by settlers.

Songs: "The Lousy Miner"

Learn More We can learn about miners during the Gold Rush by looking at primary sources. One reason so many miners stayed in California was that they could not afford to go back home. Some wrote songs about how this made them feel.

Below are the first and last verses of the song "The Lousy Miner." *Lousy* means "of poor quality." Read the words to the song and then answer the questions.

1. Underline how long the lousy miner has been looking for gold.
Identify

2. What words would you use to tell how the miner feels about leaving home? *Analyze*

_____

_____

_____

_____

The Lousy Miner

It's four long years since I reached this land,
In search of gold among the rocks and sand;
And yet I'm poor, when the truth is told,
I'm a lousy miner,
I'm a lousy miner in search of shining gold.

Oh, land of gold, you did me deceive,
And I intend in thee my bones to leave;
So farewell home, now my friends grow cold,
I'm a lousy miner,
I'm a lousy miner in search of shining gold.

— from *The Original California Songster,*
published by John A. Stone in 1855

H-SS 3.3.3 Trace why their community was established, how individuals and families contributed to its founding and development, and how the community has changed over time, drawing on maps, photographs, oral histories, letters, newspapers, and other primary sources.

How have people helped places in your region grow?

SET THE SCENE What do you know about the beginnings of California's towns and cities? For example, San Diego began as a mission. How did individuals and families who came before you help shape the place you now call home?

Preview the Lesson

Vocabulary

community *(n.)* a place where people live, work, and have fun together

founded *(v.)* started

Vocabulary Activity Circle the word above that is a synonym for *neighborhood*.

People

Junípero Serra

◉ Reading: Sequence

Remember that *sequence* is the order in which events take place. Sometimes you do not have dates to help you find the sequence of events. You will need to look for words such as *first* and *later* to help you find the order of events. Circle these words as you read page 78.

1769 Father Junípero Serra founds a mission in San Diego.

The First Towns

People started communities in California for different reasons. A **community** is a place where people live, work, and have fun together. Some communities started as missions. Father Junípero Serra [hoo NEE pay ro SAYR rah] **founded,** or started, the first mission in what is now California in San Diego in 1769. He later founded eight more of the twenty-one missions. Many of these grew into towns.

Serra's Missions

San Francisco de Asís
Santa Clara de Asís
San Carlos Borromeo de Carmelo
San Antonio de Padua
San Luís Obispo de Tolosa
San Buenaventura
San Gabriel Arcangel
San Juan Capistrano
PACIFIC OCEAN
San Diego de Alcalá

N

0   100   200 Miles
0   100   200 Kilometers

Circle the mission that Father Serra founded in 1769.

Junípero Serra founded the mission in San Diego on July 16, 1769.

1. Sequence **Write the sequence of events to match the order in which missions grew into towns.**

1st event

_____

_____

2nd event

_____

_____

3rd event

_____

_____

This is how the Camarillo family's ranch looked in 1895.

This is what a neighborhood in Camarillo looks like today.

Families and Communities

Sometimes families also helped build communities. One of these families was the Camarillo [kah mah REE yo]. They owned Rancho Calleguas [ka YAY gwahs]. The Camarillo family gave land so that churches, a college, and a high school could be built next to their ranch. The town was named Camarillo in 1899 to honor the family. Camarillo is located in Southern California.

Camarillo has grown and changed much since 1899. The population has grown to more than 60,000 people. There are a lot more homes in Camarillo today as a result of the population growth. Also, Camarillo now has many more shops and restaurants to serve the community.

2. How did the Camarillo family help build a community?

Main Idea and Details

1869

Workers on the Union Pacific Railroad built tracks west from Omaha, Nebraska, to meet tracks of the Central Pacific in Promontory, Utah.

1869. May 10th. 1869.
GREAT EVENT
Rail Road from the Atlantic to the Pacific
GRAND OPENING
OF THE
Union Pacific
RAIL ROAD,
PLATTE VALLEY ROUTE.
PASSENGER TRAINS LEAVE
OMAHA
ON THE ARRIVAL OF TRAINS FROM THE EAST
THROUGH TO SAN FRANCISCO
In less than Four Days, avoiding the Dangers of the Sea!
Travelers for Pleasure, Health or Business
LUXURIOUS CARS & EATING HOUSES
ON THE UNION PACIFIC RAIL ROAD.
PULLMAN'S PALACE SLEEPING CARS
RUN WITH ALL THROUGH PASSENGER TRAINS.
GOLD, SILVER AND OTHER MINERS!
CHEYENNE for DENVER, CENTRAL CITY & SANTA FE
Be Sure they Read via Platte Valley or Omaha

The Transcontinental Railroad Arrives

Many other people helped California's communities grow and change. Thousands of workers came to California to help build the Central Pacific Railroad. They built tracks east from Sacramento to Promontory, Utah. In 1869 the Central Pacific became part of the first railroad to connect the East to the West. This railroad was called the transcontinental railroad.

Goods and people could get to California faster than ever before. People came to live in towns near the railroad tracks. They settled there so they could be close to the goods that came in on the train and so they could ship goods they produced.

3. What was one effect the Central Pacific Railroad had on California communities?

Cause and Effect

1899

1920 Hollywood becomes the center for our country's movie-making business.

Communities Grow

Hollywood is an area in the city of Los Angeles. It is another example of a community that has grown and changed over time. In 1887 a man named Horace Wilcox started a religious community there. However, by 1920 Hollywood had become the country's center for making movies.

The new motion picture business helped the Los Angeles area grow. Movie actors and directors came from all over the world to live and work in Los Angeles. Today, the Los Angeles area is still the center of the motion picture business.

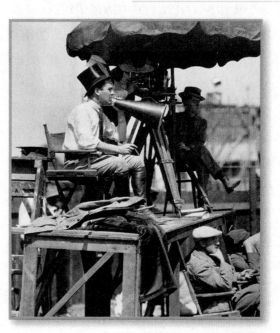

Hollywood had become the center of our country's movie-making business by 1920.

4. Why do you think the motion picture business helped the Los Angeles area grow? *Cause and Effect*

Summary

California has grown much since the time of the Spanish explorers. In what ways did early settlers help California's communities develop?

Letters: Andrew Jackson Chase

Learn More We can learn about the early history of towns and cities by studying letters. Andrew Jackson Chase moved from Stoneham, Massachusetts, to San Francisco, California, to seek his fortune during the Gold Rush. Below is a part of a letter he wrote to his brother about San Francisco in 1850. Read the passage and then answer the questions.

March 29, 1850

Your letter of Dec. 8th was received about 2 weeks ago . . . .

Although this is such a rich country in mineral wealth, I cannot advise any friend of mine to leave a comfortable home to come here—still there are brilliant prospects [chances for riches] here for the lovers of gold and many will come at all hazards [risks]. Say what we may—the gold that will be brought from the mines this season will make the world go crazy—and the growth of San Francisco is without a parallel [something similar] in history—but the ups and downs of fortunes here are equally astonishing [shocking]— there is no stability to anything . . .

1. **People from all over came to California seeking fortune. Circle descriptions of what life in California was like.** *Identify*

2. **Do you think it was easy to live in San Francisco in 1850? Why or why not?** *Analyze*

_____

_____

_____

Study Journal

In this unit you will learn how rules and laws affect our lives every day. You will also learn about how the United States government works. Complete the activities on these pages as you read the unit.

What I know about . . .

the U.S. government and the rules and laws we follow every day:

Standing Up for Beliefs

Fill in the sentences below with the correct name(s) from the word bank. There are two answers for one of the sentences.

_____ spoke out and wrote against slavery.

_____ helped write the Declaration of Independence.

_____ spoke out about her religious beliefs.

_____ led enslaved people to freedom.

_____ issued the Emancipation Proclamation.

_____ worked for civil rights.

Abraham Lincoln

Anne Hutchinson

Benjamin Franklin

Dr. Martin Luther King, Jr.

Frederick Douglass

Harriet Tubman

Thomas Jefferson

Write one fact about each symbol.

• California Flag	• U.S. flag	• Statue of Liberty

List two rights and responsibilities of citizens.

Rights	Responsibilites

List two details about each level of government in the boxes below.

City Government	California State Government	Federal Government

I have learned . . .

🐾 **H-SS 3.4.1** Determine the reasons for rules, laws, and the U.S. Constitution; the role of citizenship in the promotion of rules and laws; and the consequences for people who violate rules and laws.

How do rules and laws help people live together?

CONNECT TO YOU Drivers stopping at stop signs. Bike riders wearing helmets. These are examples of people following laws. Rules and laws help keep people safe. How do they allow people to live and work together better?

Preview the Lesson

Vocabulary

citizen *(n.)* a member of a community

right *(n.)* something that one is owed by law or custom

responsibility *(n.)* a duty, or something a person should do

obey *(v.)* to do what you are told

Vocabulary Activity Write a sentence that describes one responsibility you have at school.

_____

🔊 Reading: Cause and Effect

A *cause* tells why something happens. An *effect* tells what happens. As you read about rules and laws, ask yourself questions to look for cause and effect relationships. Write one question on the lines below.

_____

_____

Laws and the Constitution

The United States Constitution explains the powers of the national government. Only the national government can make laws for our nation. Laws protect **citizens,** or the members of a community. The Constitution also lists citizens' **rights,** or something that one is owed by law or custom. For example, it gives citizens the right to worship as they choose.

Citizens and Laws

Citizens help make laws. How? They choose the leaders who make the laws. Citizens also can tell their leaders what laws they would like to have made. Some leaders make laws for the whole country. They work at the U.S. Capitol in Washington, D.C. State leaders in Sacramento make laws for California.

1. ⟳ Cause and Effect **Use details in the text to complete the chart below.**

✎ **Cause**

The national government makes laws.

Effect

2. Underline in the text how citizens help make laws.

Main Idea and Details

The Preamble states the goals of the Constitution.

Our national lawmakers work at the Capitol Building in Washington, D.C.

Helping the Community

Good citizens feel they have a responsibility to do what is right in their community. A **responsibility** is a duty, or something a person should do. Bridget "Biddy" Mason is an example of someone who took responsibility and helped other people. In the 1800s, she got rich by buying land in Los Angeles. Then she used her money to give shelter and food to the poor.

Laws and Punishments

People must obey laws and follow rules. To **obey** is to do what you are told. Some laws tell people not to steal. Other laws say that people in cars must wear seat belts. People who do not obey laws face consequences, or the results of certain actions. One consequence is a fine, or money that must be paid to the government. People who do not wear seat belts may have to pay a fine.

3. Cause and Effect **What effect did Biddy Mason's wealth have on poor people in California?**

_____

_____

_____

Biddy Mason and the deed, or official record, of the land she bought.

4. Cause and Effect **Underline the words in the text that tell what might happen to people who do not obey laws.**

Summary

People must obey the rules and laws that the government makes. Why must people obey rules and laws?

Elizabeth Wanamaker Peratrovich, 1911–1958

Learn More Elizabeth Wanamaker Peratrovich was a member of the Tlingit Indian group. She lived in the southeastern part of what is now the state of Alaska.

When Elizabeth was a child, her parents died and she was adopted by Andrew and Mary Wanamaker. She grew up, got married, and had three children.

In 1941 Peratrovich and her family moved to Juneau, Alaska. There, Alaska Indians were not treated well. They were not allowed in many restaurants and stores. Alaska Indian children could not go to public schools. Peratrovich and her husband worked to gain rights for Alaska Indians.

In 1945 Peratrovich spoke before the leaders of the Alaska territorial government. She convinced them to pass a law so that Alaska Indians would have equal rights. Each year Alaska celebrates Elizabeth Peratrovich Day on February 16, the day that law was passed.

Answer the questions below.

1. Circle three places where Alaska Indians were not allowed in 1941. *Identify*

2. What effect did Peratrovich's work have on the Alaska Indians? *Interpret*

_____

_____

H-SS 3.4.2 Discuss the importance of public virtue and the role of citizens, including how to participate in a classroom, in the community, and in civic life.

Why is being a good citizen important?

CONNECT TO YOU An adult who gives her time to help students cross the street is a good citizen. A student who helps clean up a park is also a good citizen. Good citizens make your community a better place. Are you a good citizen?

Preview the Lesson
Vocabulary

vote *(v.)* to show your choice for something or someone

volunteer *(n.)* a person who does something without being paid or rewarded

taxes *(n.)* money the government collects to pay for its services

Vocabulary Activity Circle the vocabulary word above that describes a person who might help out in your school.

Reading: Main Idea and Details

The *main idea* tells what a paragraph is mostly about. *Details* tell more about the main idea. Underline the sentence that tells the main idea in the first paragraph on page 90.

▶

Rights of Citizens

Citizens of the United States have basic rights. These rights are described in the U.S. Constitution. Freedom of speech is one of these rights. U.S. citizens are free to say whatever they believe. They also have the right to choose their leaders.

U.S. citizens have responsibilities. They should **vote,** or show their choice for something or someone. Citizens often vote by marking a piece of paper or raising their hand. Good citizens learn about the people who want to serve in government before they vote for them. They can find out about these people by reading newspapers and listening to the news. Voting wisely helps make our cities, states, and country better.

1. Write the main idea and detail to complete the chart below. *Main Idea and Details*

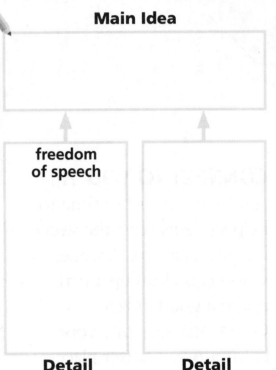

Main Idea

freedom of speech

Detail   **Detail**

Citizens vote to choose the people who serve in government.

Good citizens build strong communities.

Being a Good Citizen

People in a community show they are good citizens in many ways. They obey rules and laws. They respect the rights and property of others. Some citizens become volunteers. A **volunteer** is a person who does something without getting paid. Volunteers may shelve books at a library or help clean up a playground.

People also show they are good citizens by paying their taxes. A **tax** is money that the government collects to pay for services our community needs, such as police protection, schools, parks, and roads.

Good Citizens in the Classroom

You can be a good citizen in your classroom too. As a student you should show respect for teachers and other students. You should obey classroom rules and take part in class activities. You should help out the teacher and other students in whatever ways you can.

2. List ways volunteers are different from other workers.

Compare and Contrast

_____

_____

_____

_____

3. Underline details in the text that tell more about being a good citizen in the classroom.

Main Idea and Details

Summary

Being a good citizen is important. Name some ways you can show you are a good citizen.

Interviewing

Learn More An interview is often a meeting between two or more people to talk about something. You can interview someone in your community who volunteers. There are steps you should follow before an interview. Make a list of topics and take notes on what you want to learn. List good questions. Remember to ask: Who, What, When, Where, Why, and How. Write down or tape-record the person's answers. Be polite when you are interviewing the person. Always thank the person when you are finished.

Read the notes below for a possible interview with a volunteer. Then answer the questions.

Try It

1. Circle two topics in the notes that would help you write questions for an interview with Ms. Rodriguez. *Analyze*

2. Write two questions on the lines at the right that you would ask Ms. Rodriguez in an interview. Begin each question with Who, What, When, Where, Why, or How. *Pose Questions*

3. What should you do when you finish the interview with Ms. Rodriguez? *Identify*

Interview Notes

Ms. Rodriguez planned a project to clean up Orange Park. She asked other people to help her. Many citizens showed up to pick up litter, pull weeds, and plant flowers. Ms. Rodriguez will receive this year's Community Citizenship Award for her work.

1. Why did you decide to clean up Orange Park?

2.

3.

H-SS 3.4.3 Know the histories of important local and national landmarks, symbols, and essential documents that create a sense of community among citizens and exemplify cherished ideals (e.g., the U.S. flag, the bald eagle, the Statue of Liberty, the U.S. Constitution, the Declaration of Independence, the U.S. Capitol).

Preview the Lesson

Vocabulary

symbol *(n.)* something that stands for something else

freedom *(n.)* being able to do or say what you want without limits

pride *(n.)* a feeling of great pleasure and satisfaction in what you or someone has done

landmark *(n.)* an important building, monument, or place

heritage *(n.)* the traditional beliefs, values, and customs of a family or group

unite *(v.)* to join together

Vocabulary Activity Circle the word above that describes the feeling you would have if you did something well.

People

Thomas Jefferson
Benjamin Franklin

What brings our communities and country together?

CONNECT TO YOU Think of all the places where you see our nation's flag. You see it at schools, airports, ballparks, and many other places. How do our flag and other things that stand for the United States help bring Americans together?

Reading: Compare and Contrast

Comparing and *contrasting* things will help you look for ways they are alike and different. On page 94, underline the words that say how the U.S. flag and the California flag are alike.

▷

93

UNITED STATES
FRANCE
New York City

1782 U.S. leaders name the bald eagle our national bird.

1776 The Declaration of Independence is signed.

The American Flag

The American flag is a **symbol,** or something that stands for something else. It stands for our country, the United States. The U.S. flag has fifty stars, one for each of our fifty states. It also has thirteen red and white stripes. These stripes stand for the original, or first, thirteen English colonies, which later became states.

1. **What do the fifty stars and thirteen stripes on the U.S. flag stand for?**

Main Idea and Details

The U.S. flag (*left*) and the California state flag (*right*) are important symbols.

The California Flag

The California Bear Flag is a symbol of our state. California became a state in 1850. State lawmakers named the Bear Flag our state flag in 1911. The flag shows a brown grizzly bear, a red star, and the words California Republic. The grizzly bear is a symbol of strength. The star is taken from the Lone Star flag of Texas.

2. **Why do you think the grizzly bear is a good symbol for strength?**

Draw Conclusions

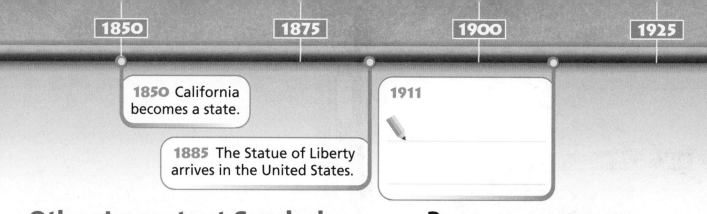

1850 California becomes a state.

1885 The Statue of Liberty arrives in the United States.

1911

Other Important Symbols

Our country's leaders chose the bald eagle as our national bird in 1782. Why did they choose this bird? Because bald eagles are independent and free. The bald eagle is a symbol of our country's strength and freedom. **Freedom** means being able to do or say what you want without limits.

The people of France gave our country a statue as a gift. The statue arrived in the United States in 1885. It shows a woman holding a torch that stands for liberty, or freedom. This statue was named the Statue of Liberty. It stands on Liberty Island in New York Harbor. Many people get a feeling of **pride,** or a feeling of great pleasure and satisfaction in what they or someone has done, when they see the Statue of Liberty.

The Statue of Liberty was completed in Paris, France, in 1884 and then sent to the United States.

3. **Why do you think the Statue of Liberty is a symbol?** *Draw Conclusions*

The Golden Gate Bridge in San Francisco was completed in 1937.

Remembering Our History

One of the ways people remember their history is by visiting landmarks. A **landmark** is an important building, monument, or place. Many landmarks are places where historical events happened. They are often preserved, or kept in their original condition. Landmarks remind people of their **heritage,** or the traditional beliefs, values, and customs of a family or group.

National and State Landmarks

There are many famous landmarks all across the United States. One is the U.S. Capitol Building in Washington, D.C. The Capitol is important because it is where our nation's lawmakers work. The President works and lives in the White House, another important landmark in Washington, D.C.

The people of California value their landmarks too. Our state's many landmarks include Spanish missions, the state capitol in Sacramento, and the Golden Gate Bridge.

4. How are landmarks and symbols different?

Compare and Contrast

_____

_____

_____

_____

5. List two famous landmarks to complete the chart below.

Compare and Contrast

Washington D.C.	California
1.	1.
2.	2.

Important Documents

Documents, or important papers, can be symbols too. They sometimes state the beliefs and values that **unite,** or join together, the people of a state or country. The Declaration of Independence is an important national document. Thomas Jefferson wrote most of it, with help from Benjamin Franklin and others. One important belief, or ideal, in the Declaration of Independence is that all people are created equal.

The U.S. Constitution and the California Constitution also state important beliefs. The U.S. Constitution includes the Bill of Rights. The Bill of Rights lists some of our basic freedoms, such as freedom of speech. The California Constitution also states this right.

6. Underline words in the text that tell how the Declaration of Independence and the U.S. Constitution are alike.

Compare and Contrast

Thomas Jefferson *(left)* wrote most of the Declaration of Independence.

Summary

Symbols such as flags, landmarks, and documents are important to our local and U.S. history. What important beliefs do our state and national symbols stand for?

The Seals of California and the United States

Learn More The state of California and the United States both have seals. A seal is an official stamp or mark that usually has a design. The California State Seal is stamped on all the laws passed in California. The seal was approved in 1849. California was the thirty-first state to join the United States. That is why our seal has thirty-one stars. The seal also has a brown grizzly bear that stands for strength. The water stands for the Pacific Ocean.

The Great Seal of the United States is stamped on documents signed by the President. It is also on one-dollar bills. This seal was approved in 1782. Its thirteen red and white stripes stand for the thirteen colonies. The blue above the stripes stands for three things: being careful, sticking with a task until it is done, and following laws so that everyone is treated fairly.

These seals show that what a document says agrees with or matches the important ideas and beliefs of the government. This is why seals are important symbols of citizenship.

Study the seals and then answer the questions below.

1. **Circle a symbol that is used in both the California and United States seals.**
   Identify

2. **Underline one sentence that tells how putting a seal on a document shows citizenship.** *Interpret*

🐻 **H-SS 3.4.4** Understand the three branches of government, with an emphasis on local government.

How does government work?

CONNECT TO YOU It takes a lot of people to run a city, state, and country. Governments have to make sure that all laws are passed and followed. How do you think the different parts of governments work together?

EQUAL JUSTICE UNDER LAW

Preview the Lesson

Vocabulary

legislator *(n.)* a member of government who helps make laws

Congress *(n.)* the lawmaking group of the U.S. government

veto *(v.)* to reject a bill that is passed by a lawmaking group

mayor *(n.)* a leader of a city or town

Vocabulary Activity Circle the words above that you would include in the category of People.

🎯 **Reading:** Cause and Effect

Looking for causes and effects can help you understand connections between events. A *cause* tells why something happens. An *effect* tells what happened. As you read page 100, underline effects that people can have on a law.

▷

Three Branches of Government

Our national government has three parts, called branches. Each branch has a different job. The legislative branch makes and changes laws. **Legislators** are members of the part of government that makes laws. **Congress** is the lawmaking group of the U.S. government. The executive branch carries out the laws. The President leads this branch. The judges of the Supreme Court head the judicial branch. They make sure that laws follow the U.S. Constitution.

Checks and Balances

Each branch of government checks and balances, or limits, what the others can do. Why? To make sure that no one branch has too much power. For example, the President can veto a bill that Congress has passed. To **veto** is to reject a bill that is passed by a lawmaking group. If Congress gets enough votes, though, it can overturn a veto. Supreme Court judges can overturn a law that both Congress and the President have agreed on.

1. **What is the judicial branch and what does it do?**

Main Idea and Details

2. Cause and Effect **What happens when the President vetoes a law or bill?**

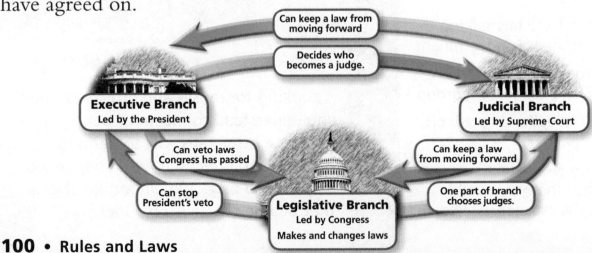

Can keep a law from moving forward

Decides who becomes a judge.

Executive Branch
Led by the President

Judicial Branch
Led by Supreme Court

Can veto laws Congress has passed

Can keep a law from moving forward

Can stop President's veto

One part of branch chooses judges.

Legislative Branch
Led by Congress
Makes and changes laws

The California State Assembly makes laws for our state.

Local Governments

City governments have parts that work together too. Every city in California has a city council. Citizens choose the members of their city council. Most city councils meet at City Hall to make local laws. They work with the city's leader. Some cities have a leader of their community called a **mayor.** In many big cities, such as Los Angeles, people elect their mayor. In some smaller cities, the city council chooses the mayor. Other cities in California may have leaders called city managers. The city council chooses this person.

City councils and city leaders work together so they can make good decisions about important local issues. For example, they often decide where to build a school or when to hire more firefighters.

3. Circle details in the text that tell more about city governments in California.

Main Idea and Details

Summary

Our national government has a structure that is different from our local government. Explain how the structures of our national and local governments are different.

Tables

Learn More Tables make information easier to read. In them, information can be put into columns that go up and down and rows that go from left to right. Labels at the top of each column group the information one way. Labels to the left of each row group the information in another way.

This table shows a schedule of city meetings for a local government. To learn when a committee meets, find that committee on the left. Then read across the row until you find the column that lists when and where that committee meets. Study the table and then answer the questions below.

Try It

1. **Circle the day, time, and place for the City Council meeting.** *Identify*

2. **Draw a box around the group that meets on Friday.** *Identify*

3. **Write a time and place for another School Board meeting on the table.** *Apply*

4. **Your family would like a dog park in your neighborhood. Underline the day, time, and place of the meeting your family would attend to present this idea.** *Analyze*

City Meetings

Group	Monday	Tuesday	Wednesday	Thursday	Friday
City Council			8–10 P.M. City Hall		
School Board		7–9 P.M. Wagner High School			
City Park Committee				2–3 P.M. Main Library	
Fine Art Commission					10–11 A.M. Smith Museum

H-SS 3.4.5 Describe the ways in which California, the other states, and sovereign American Indian tribes contribute to the making of our nation and participate in the federal system of government.

How do states, American Indians, and our country's government work together?

CONNECT TO YOU Our state has more people than any other state in the United States. Because California has so many people, it plays a big part in our country's government. How do American Indian groups contribute, or give to, our national government?

San Luis Rey
Principles of
Agreement
Signing
Ceremony

October 1 _ 02

Preview the Lesson

Vocabulary

senator *(n.)* a member of the Senate

federal *(adj.)* related to government of the whole country or national government

governor *(n.)* the top leader of a state

legislature *(n.)* a group of people who can make or change laws

Vocabulary Activity Sometimes words include other words that are close in meaning. Circle the six-letter word in *governor* in the list above. Write a short definition for it below.

Reading: Main Idea and Details

Main ideas can help you understand what a paragraph is mostly about. Sometimes writers include a topic sentence that tells the main idea. As you read the first paragraph on page 104, underline the sentence that tells the main idea. ▷

Our Nation's Government

Congress, the legislative branch of the U.S. government, is made up of leaders from our fifty states. Congress has two parts—the Senate and the House of Representatives. The Senate has 100 **senators,** or members of the Senate. Each state elects two senators. The House of Representatives has 435 members. The number of members from each state is based on the state's population. Congress is part of the **federal,** or national, government. It makes laws that are related to the government of the whole country.

State Government

State and federal governments work in ways that are similar. The **governor** is the top leader of a state. The President is the leader of our country. The **legislature** is the group of people who can make and change state laws. The California legislature has two parts, the state senate and the state assembly.

1. Write two details that support the main idea of the first paragraph.

Main Idea and Details

Main Idea

Congress is made up of leaders from our fifty states.

Detail   **Detail**

2. How are state and federal governments alike?

Compare and Contrast

_____

_____

_____

Ronald Reagan (*left*) was elected governor of California in 1966. He served as President of the United States from 1981 to 1989.

Arnold Schwarzenegger (*right*) was elected governor of California in 2003.

American Indian Governments

State and federal governments must serve the needs of American Indians by federal law. But many groups of American Indians have their own tribal governments. Each tribal government follows the federal laws too. Members of the tribal governments also choose their leaders.

A California Indian tribal government leader *(far left)* makes important decisions for his tribe, or group.

A System of Government

People in our country and American Indian tribal governments contribute to our federal system of government. For example, our two California senators represent California in the U.S. Senate. They work with the U.S. Congress to make laws about taxes, or money paid to the government for its services. The people of California and other states, including American Indian groups, pay those taxes. The federal government uses the money from these taxes to print money and to take care of national parks and monuments, among other services.

3. Based on what you have read, what do you think might happen if tribal governments did not follow state and federal laws? *Predict*

_____

_____

_____

4. Underline parts of the text that tell how American Indian groups contribute to the federal government.

Main Idea and Details

Summary

California and other states, including American Indian groups, contribute to our federal government. How are the federal, state, and tribal governments connected?

Issues and Viewpoints

Learn More Citizens vote to choose their leaders. But how do they make a choice? Good citizens pay attention to issues, or questions, that are important for leaders to decide. They can learn about the viewpoint of each person running for office. A *viewpoint* is what a person thinks about an issue. Look at each issue below and the first viewpoint. Then complete the second viewpoint. Circle the viewpoint you support.

Try It

Issue # 1: Should nine-year-olds be able to vote?

First viewpoint: No, nine-year-olds should not get to vote because they do not know enough about the people running for offices.

Second viewpoint: Yes, nine-year-olds should be able to vote because

_____

_____

Issue # 2: Should our government spend more money on playgrounds?

First viewpoint: No, our government should not spend more money on playgrounds because there are already enough playgrounds.

Second viewpoint: Yes, our government should spend more money on playgrounds because

_____

_____

H-SS 3.4.6 Describe the lives of American heroes who took risks to secure our freedoms (Anne Hutchinson, Benjamin Franklin, Thomas Jefferson, Abraham Lincoln, Frederick Douglass, Harriet Tubman, Martin Luther King, Jr.).

How have people worked for freedom?

Preview the Lesson

Vocabulary

risk *(n.)* the chance that something bad might happen

secure *(v.)* to make safe

civil rights *(n.)* the rights people have because they are citizens

Vocabulary Activity Complete the sentence below with the correct vocabulary word above.

Sometimes heroes take a _____ .

People

Anne Hutchinson
Harriet Tubman
Frederick Douglass
Abraham Lincoln
Martin Luther King, Jr.

SET THE SCENE

Have you ever helped someone? Many Americans in the past have helped others gain new rights. How do you think they reached their goals?

Reading: Cause and Effect

Remember that a *cause* tells why something happens. An *effect* tells what happens. Underline details in the first paragraph on page 108 that tell you why Anne Hutchinson moved to Boston.

1637 Anne Hutchinson is sent away for standing up for her beliefs about religion.

★ Boston

Standing Up for Beliefs

Anne Hutchinson stood up for her beliefs. In England she was not allowed to practice her religion. So she moved to Boston, Massachusetts, in 1634. She came over with other people of the same religion.

But Hutchinson's beliefs changed. She believed that faith was more important than following the rules of the church. She took a risk and told people about her beliefs. A **risk** is the chance that something bad might happen. Other people in her group wanted her to stop talking about her new beliefs. Finally, she was sent away in 1637. Today, some people think Hutchinson was a hero, or someone who acts bravely.

1. Cause and Effect **What caused Anne Hutchinson to move to Boston?**

_____

_____

Anne Hutchinson stood up for her beliefs about religion.

The Declaration of Independence was approved on July 4, 1776.

Standing Up for Freedom

Many Americans wanted to have a separate country from Great Britain during the 1700s. At that time, Great Britain ruled what is now the United States. Many people believed they would be better off if they had their own country.

Many people helped the United States become its own free country. Thomas Jefferson and Benjamin Franklin were two of these leaders. Jefferson was a wealthy farmer and lawmaker. Franklin was a scientist and inventor. Both of these men helped write the Declaration of Independence in 1776. This document gave the reasons why the United States should be free from Great Britain. Jefferson and Franklin took a risk to secure rights for the American people. To **secure** rights means to make them safe or to work hard to get them. Both men could have lost their lives for what they did.

2. Cause and Effect **What caused people to fight against Great Britain?**

Thomas Jefferson

Benjamin Franklin

PENNSYLVANIA
•Philadelphia
MARYLAND

1776 Jefferson, Franklin, and others write the Declaration of Independence.

Standing Up for Others

Harriet Tubman helped people find freedom in the 1800s. In about 1820, Tubman was born into slavery in Maryland. Slavery is the system of owning people and forcing them to work without pay. She escaped to Philadelphia, Pennsylvania, when she was an adult. She could have stayed there in safety, but she did not. She risked her freedom and her life to help other African Americans escape from slavery.

Tubman later became a leader in the Underground Railroad. The Underground Railroad was not a railroad. It was a secret group of people who helped enslaved people escape to freedom. In total, Tubman led about 300 enslaved people to freedom. No one in her care was ever caught.

3. **What happened after Harriet Tubman escaped from slavery?** Sequence

_____

_____

_____

Harriet Tubman helped enslaved people escape through the Underground Railroad.

1847

1849 Harriet Tubman escapes from slavery in Maryland.

"I stole this head, these limbs, this body from my master and ran off with them."
—Frederick Douglass

Frederick Douglass gave many speeches against slavery.

Frederick Douglass escaped from slavery, like Harriet Tubman. He also used his talents to help other enslaved people. Douglass was a writer and a speaker. He traveled to many cities and gave hundreds of speeches against slavery.

Douglass also wrote articles and three autobiographies, or books about his own life. He started his own antislavery newspaper in 1847. It was called the *North Star.* Douglass's speeches and writings reached many people. His words led other people to join the fight to stop slavery.

4. Why do you think Frederick Douglass started his own newspaper? *Draw Conclusions*

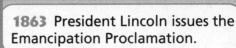
1863 President Lincoln issues the Emancipation Proclamation.

Standing Up for Our Country

President Abraham Lincoln led our country during a difficult time in U.S. history. This time was the Civil War, when the Northern states were at war against the Southern states. The Civil War started in 1861 after Southern states broke away to form their own country. They wanted to keep slavery and have more rights given to the states. The Northern states went to war with the Southern states to stop this from happening.

President Lincoln wanted to end slavery. He issued a document called the Emancipation Proclamation during the war in 1863. This document freed the enslaved people in many of the Southern states. The Northern states won the war in 1865, and slavery was ended.

5. Cause and Effect **What event freed enslaved people in the Southern states?**

_____

_____

"... all persons held as slaves within any State or designated part of a State, the people whereof shall then be in rebellion against the United States, shall be then, thenceforward, and forever free."

—from the Emancipation Proclamation

President Lincoln issued the Emancipation Proclamation on January 1, 1863.

1964

Standing Up for Rights

Dr. Martin Luther King, Jr., worked for civil rights for all people in the 1950s and 1960s. **Civil rights** are the rights people have because they are citizens. Many blacks were not allowed to vote or to go to the same schools as white people. Dr. King led many protests and spoke out against such unfairness. Many white people did not like what Dr. King was doing. He often faced great danger.

Dr. King gave one of his most famous speeches in Washington, D.C., in 1963. He said that Americans should be judged by their words and actions and not by the color of their skin. A civil rights law was finally passed in 1964 that said that all Americans have equal rights.

6. Cause and Effect **Why did Dr. Martin Luther King, Jr., lead peaceful protests?**

Summary

Many people took risks to secure rights and freedoms for all Americans. Which of these people do you think was a hero? Explain why.

Kalpana Chawla, 1961–2003

Learn More Kalpana Chawla was an astronaut with the National Aeronautics and Space Administration (NASA). She was born in India, but she moved to the United States to study.

Chawla became a U.S. citizen. She applied to be an astronaut about ten years later. NASA accepted her. Chawla was trained to be a mission specialist and perform experiments in space. In 1997 she flew on the space shuttle *Columbia*. This flight made Chawla the first Indian woman to go into space. When she flew on *Columbia* again in 2003, the shuttle had an accident. Everyone on board, including Chawla, died.

In total, Chawla spent more than thirty days in space. She received many awards for her work, including the Congressional Space Medal of Honor.

Answer the questions below.

1. **What was Chawla the first to do? Underline your answer in the text.** *Identify*

2. **Do you think that Chawla deserved the Congressional Space Medal of Honor? Why or why not?** *Analyze*

_____

_____

_____

Study Journal

In this lesson you will learn about the different types of resources and about how things are bought and sold. You will also learn how to make decisions about money. You will see how school helps you make decisions about your future. Complete the activities on these pages as you read the unit.

What I know about . . .

California's economy:

_____

Different Kinds of Resources

Fill in the three boxes below with a detail that tells more about each kind of resource.

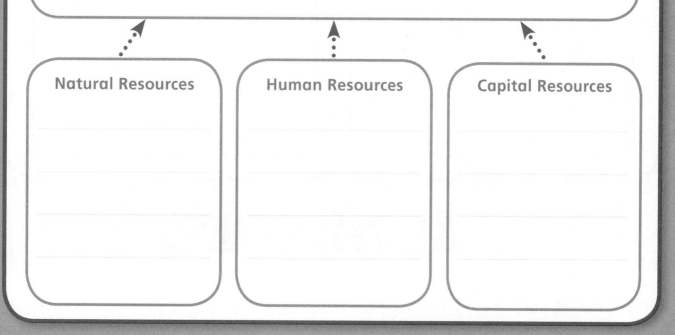

Producers use three kinds of resources to produce goods and services.

Natural Resources	Human Resources	Capital Resources

Complete the sentences below. Then list two examples of each.

A need is _____

_____

1. _____

2. _____

A want is _____

_____

1. _____

2. _____

Choose one of the wants from your list above. Write three steps to plan for how you might be able to save money to buy it.

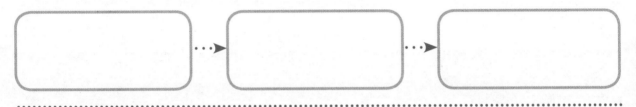

···

Think about what you want to do in the future. Write it in the space called My Future. In the space called Now, list two choices you will need to make in school now to prepare for your future.

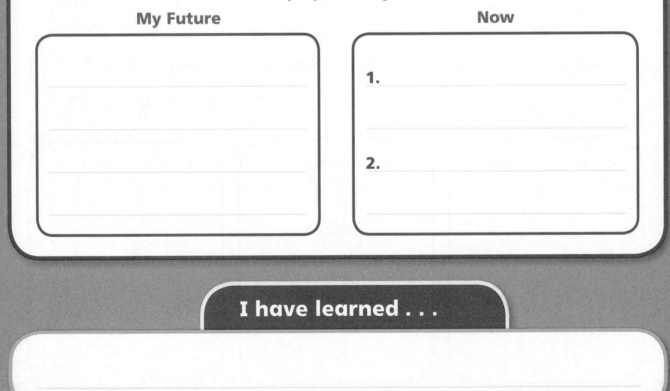

My Future	Now
	1. _____
	_____
	2. _____
	_____

I have learned . . .

_____

_____

H-SS 3.5.1 Describe the ways in which local producers have used and are using natural resources, human resources, and capital resources to produce goods and services in the past and the present.

What kinds of resources do we use?

CONNECT TO YOU What resources do we use to meet our needs? Trees, soil, wind, and water are some resources that we use. But did you know that people can also be a resource?

Preview the Lesson

Vocabulary

producer *(n.)* a person or business that makes things

consumer *(n.)* a person who uses or buys goods and services

Vocabulary Activity One meaning of the suffix *-er* is someone who does something. Underline the words in the definitions above that tell what the person does.

People

César Chávez

Reading: Predict

To *predict* means to think about what might happen before it happens based on what you already know. Circle below what you predict you will be reading about in this lesson.

government   **natural resources**   **explorers**

▶

Borax is a mineral found in southeastern California. Borax can be used to make glass and soap.

California's Natural Resources

California is rich in natural resources. A natural resource is a useful material that occurs in nature. A few of these resources are wood, gemstones, oil, and minerals.

Producers use natural resources. A **producer** is a person or business that makes things. For example, producers use wood from forests to make lumber and paper. Producers also use minerals. Minerals are natural substances found in the earth. Minerals can be in solid or liquid form. Some minerals found in our state are gold, copper, borax, and tungsten. Tungsten is used to make light bulbs.

A business can also act as a producer. Businesses in the United States produce and sell goods to other countries.

1. Predict **What do you think might happen if we used all of our natural resources?**

Other Resources

Other types of resources are human resources and capital resources. Human resources are workers who produce goods and provide services. Many people in California work in service businesses, such as stores, offices, hospitals, and other places. Capital resources are the machines, tools, and buildings that are used to produce goods and services. In the past, many products were made by hand. Today, machines help make products more quickly.

The goods that workers produce and the services they provide are used by consumers. A **consumer** is a person who uses or buys goods and services.

2. How are human resources different from natural resources?

Compare and Contrast

All kinds of workers are human resources.

Teacher

Woodworker

Store clerk

Caring for Our Resources

The Earth has only a limited amount of some natural resources. The California Indians who lived here before the settlers came used only the resources they needed. They did not hunt or fish for more than they could use.

People use more resources today. We can conserve these natural resources so they will last longer. When we conserve resources, we use them carefully. One way to conserve natural resources is to use less of them. People also conserve resources by replanting trees, by not overusing soil, and by passing laws to protect resources. In fact, they can recycle paper, glass, plastic, and aluminum containers.

3. List two ways people can take care of our natural resources.

Main Idea and Details

Some materials can be recycled and made into new products.

WE RECYCLE

Treating Workers Fairly

We need to care for our human resources too. A man named César Chávez saw that many farm owners in our state did not pay their workers fairly. The owners often made many workers do dangerous work. So Chávez and Dolores Huerta worked in the 1960s and 1970s to start a labor union for farm workers. A labor union is a group that makes sure workers are treated fairly.

4. Underline the reasons why César Chávez and Dolores Huerta started a labor union for farm workers.

Cause and Effect

Dolores Huerta and César Chávez led the United Farm Workers convention in Fresno in 1973.

Summary

Producers have used and are using resources to produce goods and services. Name the three different types of resources and tell how they are used.

Fact and Fiction

Learn More One important thing to know when you are reading is whether what you are reading is fact or fiction. A fact is a statement that is often believed to be true. Facts usually can be proved to be true by checking in a dictionary or encyclopedia. Fiction is a story that is made up. The characters or events in fiction may seem real. But they were created by a writer to tell a story.

The first passage below is taken from your text. The second passage is not from your text. Read them both and then answer the questions.

Try It

1. **Underline the words that tell you which passage is fiction.** *Identify*

2. **Circle the words in the other passage that are facts.** *Identify*

3. **Write a sentence to add to the end of passage #2.** *Apply*

_____

_____

4. **Explain why it is important to know the difference between fact and fiction.** *Analyze*

_____

_____

Passage #1

One way to conserve natural resources is to use less of them. People also conserve resources by replanting trees, by not overusing soil, and by passing laws to protect resources. In fact, they can recycle paper, glass, plastic, and aluminum containers.

Passage #2

Tony and Ana did not want their resources to run out. So they built a special box. In it they put every resource they could find. They hoped the box would not burst with all of the resources. They wanted to save the resources to use later.

H-SS 3.5.2 Understand that some goods are made locally, some elsewhere in the United States, and some abroad.

Where are goods made?

CONNECT TO YOU
Think about what you ate for breakfast. Did you have cereal, toast, eggs, or something else? Food and other products can be made here or elsewhere.

Preview the Lesson
Vocabulary

import *(n.)* a product or resource that is brought into one country from another

export *(n.)* a product or resource that is sent to another country to be sold

Vocabulary Activity Underline the words in the definitions of *import* and *export* that make them different.

Reading: Main Idea and Details

Remember that the *main idea* is the most important idea in a paragraph. Underline the sentence that tells the main idea in the first paragraph on page 124.

Local Goods

All kinds of goods are produced in our state. Grapes, cotton, almonds, tomatoes, milk, and eggs are some of the crops and food products that are produced here. Other products, such as those made with minerals, are produced through mining.

Tomatoes are one of our state's most important farm products.

1. What kinds of goods are produced in our state?

Main Idea and Details

Goods from Other Places

Many goods that we use are produced right here in California. But we also use goods that come from other places around the country. We might eat potatoes from Idaho, maple syrup from Vermont, or apples from Washington. We might also enjoy goods from around the world. We might buy cheese from France, bananas from Costa Rica, or toys from China. Many goods produced in our state are sent to other places throughout the country and around the world.

2. What are some goods that other states produce?

Main Idea and Details

People in California can enjoy apples from Washington.

World's Finest!

Washington STATE Apples

Producing Goods to Sell

Most places or regions cannot produce all the goods or services that people need. So people in regions trade with each other. When people from different regions trade, they buy or sell goods and services. There are important reasons for trading. A region may not be able to produce what it needs. Or goods might cost less somewhere else.

Trade with Other Places

People in countries and states often trade with each other. For example, people in the United States trade with people in countries such as Canada, Japan, and Mexico. A product or resource that a country brings in from another country is an **import.** An **export** is a product or resource that is sent to another country to be sold. The United States imports cars, computers, clothes, and oil. Our country exports cars, airplanes, and food.

Many goods come into California by ship through the Port of San Francisco.

3. **Why would people in different regions need to trade goods?**
Cause and Effect

_____

_____

_____

4. **Circle exports the United States sends to other countries.** *Main Idea and Details*

Summary

Many goods we use are made in our community or in our state. Other goods are made far away. How are goods exchanged between California and other places?

Bar Graphs

Learn More A bar graph shows how certain information can be compared. The bar graph below shows some of the farm products that were exported from California in 2001. The height or length of each bar represents a number. That number stands for a farm export's value in millions of dollars.

Look at the bar graph to find a farm export. Follow the line at the top of the bar to the numbers at the left. That number will tell you the value of that farm export in millions of dollars. Use the bar graph to answer the questions below.

Try It

1. Which farm export had the highest value in dollars in 2001? *Identify*

_____

2. What was the value of cotton exports in 2001? *Apply*

_____

3. Circle the farm export that had a value of about $200 million in 2001. *Apply*

4. Draw a star above the two farm exports that had about the same value in 2001. *Interpret*

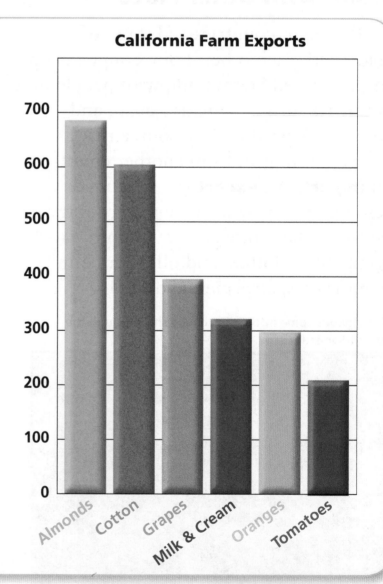

California Farm Exports

Source: CA Department of Food and Agriculture, 2001

H-SS 3.5.3 Understand that individual economic choices involve trade-offs and the evaluation of benefits and costs.

How do we decide what we want?

CONNECT TO YOU Do you ever have a hard time knowing what to do with your money? You may want to spend it on something you want. Or you may want to save it to buy something later. Why do you think learning how to spend and save money wisely is important?

Preview the Lesson

Vocabulary

earn *(v.)* to get money in exchange for work

choice *(n.)* picking between two or more things

savings *(n.)* the amount of money you earn but do not spend

income *(n.)* all the money a person gets from work or other sources

budget *(n.)* a plan that shows income, spending, and saving

Vocabulary Activity Write a sentence below that describes how you earn money.

_____

_____

Reading: Cause and Effect

Sometimes writers use *cause-and-effect* words to help you understand what happened and why. One cause-and-effect signal word is *because*. Underline the word when you see it on page 129. ▶

Making, Spending, and Saving

People need to earn money in order to have money to spend. To **earn** is to get money in exchange for work.

Using money means making a **choice,** or picking between two or more things. You can choose to spend money now or to put it in savings. **Savings** is the amount of money that you earn but do not spend. If you save your money, the trade-off is that you will have the money to buy something you want or need later.

Needs and Wants

When people spend money, they get something in return. People often have to make choices between needs and wants. Needs are things people must have. All people need food, clothes, and a place to live. Wants are things people would like to have but do not need. You may want a video game, a basketball, or a piece of jewelry. Your friends may want something else. Wants are choices. Different people might want different things.

1. **Why do people put money in savings?** *Cause and Effect*

2. **Is a bike a need or a want? Explain your answer.**

Draw Conclusions

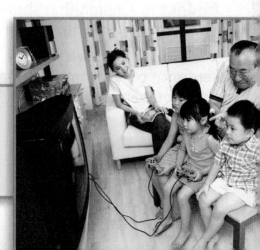

People make choices between needs and wants. Food is a need. A video game is a want.

Keeping Track of Spending

Many people need to be careful about how they spend money. They have to make sure they do not spend more than their income. **Income** is all the money a person gets from work or another source. Many people follow a budget to make good choices about spending money. A **budget** is a plan that shows income, spending, and savings. You might need to have a budget because without it you might spend too much money.

My Budget			
Week	Income	Spending	Savings
Week 1	$6.00	$1.00	$5.00
Week 2	$6.00	$1.00	$5.00
Week 3	$6.00	$1.00	$5.00
Week 4	$6.00	$1.00	$5.00
Week 5	$6.00	$1.00	$5.00
Week 6	$6.00	$1.00	$5.00
Week 7	$6.00	$1.00	$5.00
Total	$42.00	$7.00	$35.00

Pedro wants to buy a video game, so he makes a budget. His income is $6 a week from doing chores at home. If he spends $1 a week, he will save $5 a week. The video game costs $35. How many weeks will it take for Pedro to save for the video game?

3. **Why do people need a budget?** *Cause and Effect*

_____

_____

_____

Summary

People can make wise money choices by thinking about their wants and needs and about trade-offs. If a person spends all of his or her money on one thing, what trade-off does that person make?

Decision Making

Learn More You probably make decisions about choices every day. Following a step-by-step plan can help you make a good decision.

Suppose that you really wanted to buy a new bicycle helmet. The helmet costs $25. You have saved $15. You need $10 more to buy the helmet. But then you see a T-shirt you have wanted. It is $15. Do you spend your savings on the T-shirt, or do you wait and save the money until you have enough for the helmet? Use the chart below to answer the questions and help you make a decision.

Try It

1. **What will happen if you buy the T-shirt now?**

   Interpret

   _____

   _____

   _____

2. **Which do you think is the better decision? Explain your answer.**

   Analyze

   _____

   _____

   _____

   _____

Decision-Making Chart

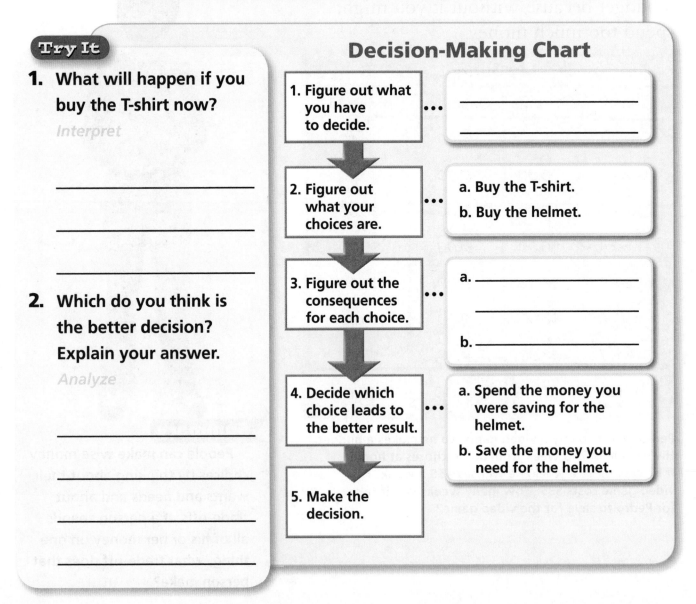

1. Figure out what you have to decide. ··· _____ _____

2. Figure out what your choices are. ··· a. Buy the T-shirt. b. Buy the helmet.

3. Figure out the consequences for each choice. ··· a. _____ _____ b. _____

4. Decide which choice leads to the better result. ··· a. Spend the money you were saving for the helmet. b. Save the money you need for the helmet.

5. Make the decision.

H-SS 3.5.4 Discuss the relationship of students' "work" in school and their personal human capital.

How does your work in school help you?

CONNECT TO YOU What work do you want to do when you grow up? You could do just about anything. It is up to you. How will your work in school help you make good choices for your future?

Preview the Lesson

Vocabulary

prepare *(v.)* to make ready

effort *(n.)* the energy needed to do something

Vocabulary Activity Underline the word above that describes something you would do before a trip.

People

Jaime Escalante

⊙ Reading: Predict

To *predict* means to think about what might happen before it happens based on what you already know. Before you read page 132, look at the photograph and caption to predict why choices in school are important to your future.

▶

Making Choices

You will decide over time what you want to do when you grow up. You will decide where you will live, who your friends are, and what job you do. A good way to start making these choices is to think about what you like to do and what you do well. It also helps to learn about all of your choices. A good place to learn about choices is in school.

What we learn about in school can help us to become successful.

Education Is Important

Education helps prepare you for your future. To **prepare** means to make ready. You go to school to learn the things that you need to know to be successful in life. Being successful may mean having a good job, raising a family, and being a good citizen. Our country's leaders want people to have a good education. This is why every child in California has the right to a free education.

1. 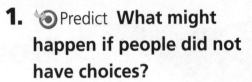 Predict **What might happen if people did not have choices?**

2. How does an education prepare you for the future?

Main Idea and Details

Jobs for the Future

One important choice we all have to make is what we want for our future. Whatever you want to do, you can start preparing now. The subjects you learn in school can help you do many different jobs. For example, doctors need math to help them give people the right amount of medicine. Parents need math to keep a family budget. Builders need math to build a house.

Parent

Construction worker

Reading is an important skill for every job.

Doctor

It Takes Energy

The effort that you make now to do well in school will help you later on. **Effort** means the energy needed to do something. It may affect what kind of job you have. It may also affect how much money you will make.

3. ⟳ Predict **What school subjects do you predict will help you in the future?**

_____

_____

_____

4. **Underline the future effects of putting effort into learning now.**

Cause and Effect

Summary

Education can help you make good choices and prepare you for your life ahead. How can the work you do in school now help you in the future?

Jaime Escalante, b. 1930

Learn More Jaime Escalante likes teaching. He was a math teacher in Bolivia, a country in South America. But when he moved to the United States, Escalante could not speak English. He worked as a janitor so he could go to college at night. Escalante studied science and math and learned how to speak English. After he graduated from college, he became a high school teacher in Los Angeles.

Escalante expected all of his students to work hard. How was Escalante successful? He believed in his students. He knew they could learn if they made the effort. Escalante also made math more fun by comparing it to activities such as basketball. The 1988 movie *Stand and Deliver* tells about the success of Escalante and his students.

Answer the questions below.

1. **Underline the names of three subjects that Escalante studied in college.** *Identify*

2. **Name one way that Escalante helped his students do well.** *Interpret*

_____

_____

_____

Reference Guide

Table of Contents

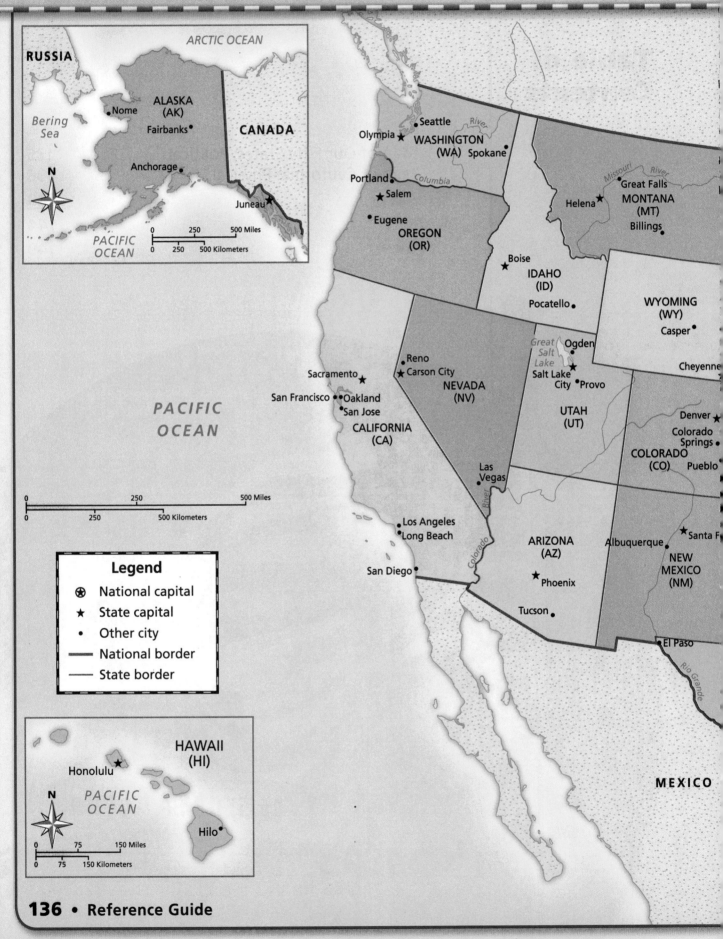

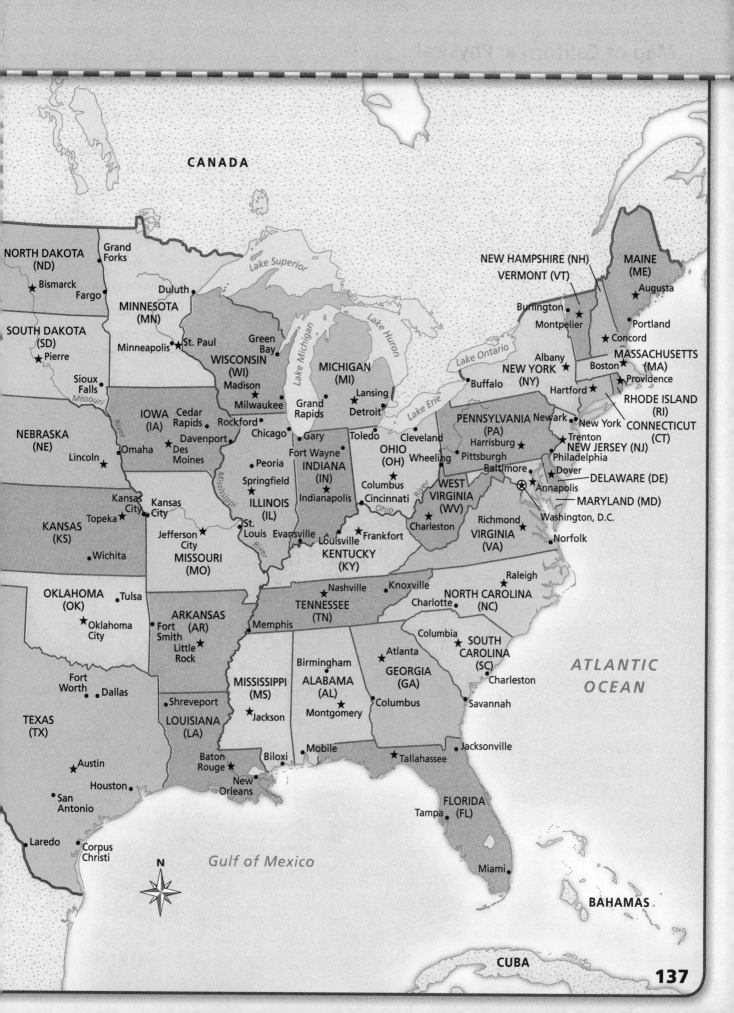

CANADA

NORTH DAKOTA (ND)
Grand Forks
Bismarck
Fargo

SOUTH DAKOTA (SD)
Pierre
Sioux Falls

Lake Superior

MINNESOTA (MN)
Duluth
Minneapolis
St. Paul
Missouri River

NEBRASKA (NE)
Omaha
Lincoln

Green Bay
WISCONSIN (WI)
Madison
Milwaukee

IOWA (IA)
Cedar Rapids
Davenport
Des Moines
Rockford

KANSAS (KS)
Kansas City
Topeka
Wichita

Lake Michigan
MICHIGAN (MI)
Grand Rapids
Lansing
Detroit
Lake Huron

Chicago
Gary
ILLINOIS (IL)
Peoria
Springfield
St. Louis
Evansville

INDIANA (IN)
Fort Wayne
Indianapolis

Toledo
OHIO (OH)
Columbus
Cincinnati
Cleveland
Wheeling
Lake Erie

Lake Ontario

NEW HAMPSHIRE (NH)
VERMONT (VT)
Burlington
Montpelier

MAINE (ME)
Augusta
Portland
Concord

NEW YORK (NY)
Albany
Buffalo

MASSACHUSETTS (MA)
Boston
Providence
Hartford
RHODE ISLAND (RI)
CONNECTICUT (CT)

PENNSYLVANIA (PA)
Harrisburg
Pittsburgh
Newark
New York
Trenton
NEW JERSEY (NJ)
Philadelphia
Dover
DELAWARE (DE)
Baltimore
Annapolis
MARYLAND (MD)
Washington, D.C.

WEST VIRGINIA (WV)
Charleston
Ohio River

VIRGINIA (VA)
Richmond
Norfolk

MISSOURI (MO)
Jefferson City

Mississippi River

KENTUCKY (KY)
Louisville
Frankfort

OKLAHOMA (OK)
Tulsa
Oklahoma City

ARKANSAS (AR)
Fort Smith
Little Rock

TENNESSEE (TN)
Nashville
Memphis
Knoxville

NORTH CAROLINA (NC)
Raleigh
Charlotte

Columbia
SOUTH CAROLINA (SC)
Charleston

ATLANTIC OCEAN

TEXAS (TX)
Fort Worth
Dallas
Austin
Houston
San Antonio
Laredo
Corpus Christi

MISSISSIPPI (MS)
Jackson
Shreveport
LOUISIANA (LA)
Baton Rouge
New Orleans

ALABAMA (AL)
Birmingham
Montgomery
Columbus
Mobile
Biloxi

GEORGIA (GA)
Atlanta
Savannah
Jacksonville
Tallahassee

FLORIDA (FL)
Tampa
Miami

N

Gulf of Mexico

BAHAMAS

CUBA

137

Atlas
Map of California: Physical

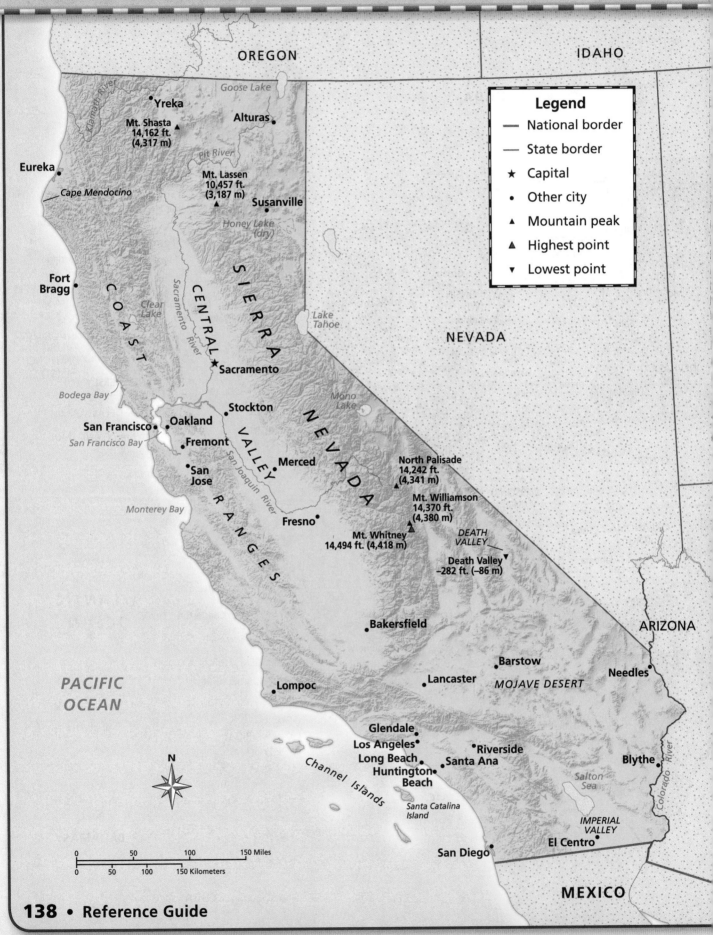

OREGON

IDAHO

Goose Lake

Yreka

Alturas

Mt. Shasta
14,162 ft.
(4,317 m)

Klamath River

Pit River

Legend
— National border
— State border
★ Capital
● Other city
▲ Mountain peak
▲ Highest point
▼ Lowest point

Eureka

Cape Mendocino

Mt. Lassen
10,457 ft.
(3,187 m)

Susanville

Honey Lake
(dry)

S I E R R A

Fort
Bragg

C O A S T

Clear
Lake

Sacramento River

C E N T R A L

Lake
Tahoe

NEVADA

Bodega Bay

★ Sacramento

Stockton

Mono
Lake

San Francisco

Oakland

Fremont

V A L L E Y

N E V A D A

San Francisco Bay

San
Jose

Merced

San Joaquin River

North Palisade
14,242 ft.
(4,341 m)

Mt. Williamson
14,370 ft.
(4,380 m)

Monterey Bay

R A N G E S

Fresno

Mt. Whitney
14,494 ft. (4,418 m)

DEATH
VALLEY

Death Valley
−282 ft. (−86 m)

ARIZONA

Bakersfield

Barstow

Needles

PACIFIC
OCEAN

Lompoc

Lancaster

MOJAVE DESERT

Glendale

Los Angeles

Riverside

Blythe

Long Beach

Santa Ana

Colorado River

Channel Islands

Huntington
Beach

Salton
Sea

N

Santa Catalina
Island

IMPERIAL
VALLEY

El Centro

San Diego

MEXICO

0   50   100   150 Miles
0   50   100   150 Kilometers

Glossary

This glossary will help you understand the meanings of and pronounce the vocabulary words in this book. The page number tells you where the word first appears.

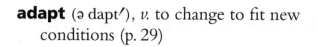

adapt (ə dapt′), *v.* to change to fit new conditions (p. 29)

budget (buj′it), *n.* a plan that shows income, spending, and saving (p. 127)

C

canal (kə nal′), *n.* a narrow waterway that has been dug across land (p. 9)

ceremony (ser′ə mō′nē), *n.* an important activity done for a special reason (p. 17)

choice (chois), *n.* picking between two or more things (p. 127)

citizen (sit′ə zən), *n.* a member of a community (p. 85)

civil rights (siv′əl rīts), *n.* the rights people have because they are citizens (p. 107)

climate (klī′mit), *n.* the weather an area usually has year after year (p. 29)

community (kə myü′nə tē), *n.* a place where people live, work, and have fun together (p. 77)

conflict (kon′flikt), *n.* a struggle or disagreement (p. 53)

Congress (kong′gris), *n.* the lawmaking group of the U.S. government (p. 99)

constitution (kon′stə tü′shən), *n.* a written plan for a government (p. 41)

consumer (kən sü′mər), *n.* a person who uses or buys goods and services (p. 117)

cooperate (kō op′ə rāt′), *v.* to work together (p. 53)

culture (kul′chər), *n.* the arts, beliefs, behavior, and ideas of a group of people (p. 67)

custom (kus′təm), *n.* a way of doing things (p. 17)

Pronunciation Key

a	in hat	ō	in open	sh	in she
ā	in age	ȯ	in all	th	in thin
â	in care	ô	in order	ᴛʜ	in then
ä	in far	oi	in oil	zh	in measure
e	in let	ou	in out	ə	= a in about
ē	in equal	u	in cup	ə	= e in taken
ėr	in term	u̇	in put	ə	= i in pencil
i	in it	ü	in rule	ə	= o in lemon
ī	in ice	ch	in child	ə	= u in circus
o	in hot	ng	in long		

Glossary

D

dam (dam), *n.* a wall built to hold back water (p. 9)

E

earn (èrn), *v.* to get money in exchange for work (p. 127)

economy (i kon′ə mē), *n.* the way things are made and are bought and sold in a country, region, state, or local area (p. 41)

effort (ef′ərt), *n.* the energy needed to do something (p. 131)

environment (en vī′rən mənt), *n.* the land, water, and air in which people, animals, and plants live (p. 9)

explorer (ek splôr′ər), *n.* someone who travels to new places to learn more about them (p. 67)

export (ek′spôrt), *n.* a product or resource that is sent to another country to be sold (p. 123)

F

federal (fed′ər əl), *adj.* related to government of the whole country or national government (p. 103)

flood (flud), *n.* a sudden flow of water that covers what is normally dry land (p. 9)

folklore (fōk′lôr′), *n.* the stories and customs of a group of people (p. 17)

founded (found′əd), *v.* started (p. 77)

freedom (frē′dəm), *n.* being able to do or say what you want without limits (p. 93)

G

geography (jē og′rə fē), *n.* the surface features of a place (p. 3)

good (gùd), *n.* a thing that is made or grown and then sold (p. 73)

government (guv′ərn mənt), *n.* the people who run a state or country, or the laws of a state or country (p. 41)

governor (guv′ərn), *n.* the top leader of a state (p. 103)

H

heritage (her′ə tij), *n.* the traditional beliefs, values, and customs of a family or group (p. 93)

Glossary

I

import (im′pôrt), *n.* a product or resource that is brought into one country from another (p. 123)

income (in′kum′), *n.* all the money a person gets from work or other sources (p. 127)

interact (in′tər akt′), *v.* to talk to other people and work with them (p. 53)

L

laborer (lā′bər ər), *n.* a worker (p. 73)

landmark (land′märk′), *n.* an important building, monument, or place (p. 93)

laws (loz), *n.* rules made by a government (p. 41)

legislator (lej′ə slā′tər), *n.* a member of government who helps make laws (p. 99)

legislature (lej′ə slā′chər), *n.* a group of people who can make or change laws (p. 103)

M

mayor (mā′ər), *n.* a leader of a city or town (p. 99)

mission (mish′ən), *n.* a settlement set up by a religious group to teach religion and other ways of life to native people (p. 53)

O

obey (ō bā′), *v.* to do what you are told (p. 85)

ownership (ō′nər ship), *n.* having something that belongs only to you (p. 73)

P

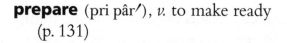

prepare (pri pâr′), *v.* to make ready (p. 131)

pride (prīd), *n.* a feeling of great pleasure and satisfaction in what you or someone has done (p. 93)

producer (prə dü′sər), *n.* a person or business that makes things (p. 117)

Pronunciation Key		
a in hat	ō in open	sh in she
ā in age	ȯ in all	th in thin
â in care	ô in order	ŦH in then
ä in far	oi in oil	zh in measure
e in let	ou in out	ə = a in about
ē in equal	u̇ in cup	ə = e in taken
ėr in term	u̇ in put	ə = i in pencil
i in it	ü in rule	ə = o in lemon
ī in ice	ch in child	ə = u in circus
o in hot	ng in long	

Glossary

property (prop′ər tē), *n.* a thing someone owns (p. 73)

protect (prə tekt′), *v.* to keep someone or something safe (p. 9)

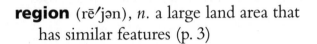

region (rē′jən), *n.* a large land area that has similar features (p. 3)

religion (ri lij′ən), *n.* a system of faith and worship (p. 53)

reservation (rez′ər vā′shən), *n.* an area of land owned by an American Indian group (p. 41)

resource (rē′sôrs or ri sôrs′), *n.* anything that meets people's needs (p. 9)

responsibility (ri spon′sə bil′ə tē), *n.* a duty, or something a person should do (p. 85)

right (rīt), *n.* something that one is owed by law or custom (p. 85)

risk (risk), *n.* the chance that something bad might happen (p. 107)

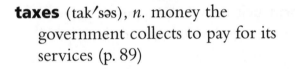

savings (sā′ving), *n.* the amount of money you earn but do not spend (p. 127)

secure (si kyür′), *v.* to make safe (p. 107)

senator (sen′ə tər), *n.* a member of the Senate (p. 103)

service (sėr′vis), *n.* a job that someone does for others and for which he or she is usually paid (p. 73)

settler (set′lər), *n.* someone who goes to live in a new place (p. 53)

symbol (sim′bəl), *n.* something that stands for something else (p. 93)

taxes (tak′səs), *n.* money the government collects to pay for its services (p. 89)

tradition (trə dish′ən), *n.* a special way a group of people does something and that has been passed on to others (p. 17)

unite (yü nīt′), *v.* to join together (p. 93)

Glossary

V

veto (vē′tō), *v.* to reject a bill that is passed by a lawmaking group (p. 99)

volunteer (vol′ən tir′), *n.* a person who does something without being paid or rewarded (p. 89)

vote (vōt), *v.* to show your choice for something or someone (p. 89)

W

weather (weŦH′ər), *n.* the temperature and conditions of the air outside at a certain place and time (p. 29)

Pronunciation Key					
a	in hat	ō	in open	sh	in she
ā	in age	ȯ	in all	th	in thin
â	in care	ô	in order	ŦH	in then
ä	in far	oi	in oil	zh	in measure
e	in let	ou	in out	ə	= a in about
ē	in equal	u	in cup	ə	= e in taken
ėr	in term	u̇	in put	ə	= i in pencil
i	in it	ü	in rule	ə	= o in lemon
ī	in ice	ch	in child	ə	= u in circus
o	in hot	ng	in long		

Index

This Index lists the pages on which topics appear in this book. Page numbers after an *m* refer to a map. The terms *See* and *See also* will direct you to more entries.

Index

Index

Index

Index

Credits

Text

Excerpt from 'Diary of Pedro Font', December 7, 1775 & February 24, 1776 from *Anza's California Expeditions 5 vols.* Copyright © 1930 The Regents of the University of California. Reprinted by permission. p. 56

Illustrations

9 Jane Chambless Wright; **8, 14, 18, 19, 32, 36, 42, 68, 74, 78, 80, 94, 108, 110, 112, 136, 138** Mapquest, Inc.; **10** (Johnny) Laura Logan, (map) Mapquest, Inc.; **11** Sarah Dillard; **23, 33, 47, 64** Toby Williams; **27, v** Burgandy Beam; **46** Joe LeMonnier.

Photographs

Every effort has been made to secure permission and provide appropriate credit for photographic material. The publisher deeply regrets any omission and pledges to correct errors called to its attention in subsequent editions.

Unless otherwise acknowledged, all photographs are the property of Pearson Education, Inc.

Photo locators denoted as follows: Top (T), Center (C), Bottom (B), Left (L), Right (R), Background (Bkgd)

Front Matter: i (T) ©Harald Sund/Getty Images, (C) Harvey Lloyd/Getty Images; **ii** (T) Michael DeFreitas North America/Alamy Stock Photo, (C) ©Douglas Stone; **iii** (T) Alexander Zavadsky/Shutterstock, (C) Rachel Epstein/PhotoEdit; **iv** (T) Uladzik Kryhin/Shutterstock, (T) ©Museum of Ventura County; **v** (C) Paul Marcus/Shutterstock, (C) ©David Young-Wolff/PhotoEdit; **vi** (Bkgd) ©Spencer Grant/PhotoEdit.

Unit 1: 3 ©DK Images; **4** (Bkgd) ©Harald Sund/Getty Images; **5** (C) ©Tony Craddock/Getty Images; **9** Andresr/E+/Getty Images; **10** Karsten Hennig/Action Press/ZUMAPRESS.com; **11** (B) Shasta Dam/123RF; **12** (B) Trekandshoot/Alamy Stock Photo; **13** (R) Michael Fitzsimmons/ShutterstocK' Library of Congress/RGB Ventures/SuperStock/Alamy Stock Photo;

Unit 2: 17 Inga spence/Alamy Stock Photo, (CR) ©Spencer Grant/PhotoEdit; **20** Lisa Werner/Alamy Stock Photo; **21** (BL) Grandriver/E+/Getty Images; **22** Exactostock/SuperStock; **24** (B) World History Archive/Alamy Stock Photo, (TR) ©Jerry E. Ross/Nature Picture Library, (T) Archive PL/Alamy

Stock Photo, (BL) Phoebe A. Hearst Museum of Anthropology; **25** (B) Granger, NYC, (B) David MCnew/AFP/Getty Images, (TL) Phoebe A. Hearst Museum of Anthropology, (T) ©Renee Lynn/Getty Images; **26** (T) ©Bob Rowan; Progressive Image/Corbis, (T) ©Kim Westerskov/Getty Images, (BR) age fotostock/SuperStock, (TL, BC) Shutterstock; **27** (T) ©Bill Freeman/PhotoEdit, (TL) ©Fotofermer/Fotolia, (B) Jack Goldfarb/VIBE/Design Pics Inc/Alamy Stock Photo, (BR) Aram Williams/Alamy Images; **29** (C) Michael DeFreitas North America/Alamy Stock Photo; **30** (B) ©Prints & Photographs Division, Edward S. Curtis Collection, [reproduction number: LC-USZ62-98674]/Library of Congress; **31** SuperStock; **33** (B) ©Adam Jones/Getty Images, (B) ©Andrew Ward/Life File/Getty Images, (B) Mariusz S. Jurgielewicz/Shutterstock, (BL) George Ostertag/Purestock /SuperStock; **34** (BR) Corbis/SuperStock, (TR) Edward S. Curtis Collection/Prints & Photographs Division, Library of Congress, (T) Wildlife GmbH/Alamy Stock Photo; **35** (C) Gary Tognoni/123RF, (TR) Nancy Carter/North Wind Picture Archives; **36** (C) Arco Images GmbH/Arco / O. Diez/Alamy Stock Photo, (BL) ©George D. Lepp/Corbis, (B) ©Hal Beral/Corbis, (TR) John Elk/Lonely Planet Images/Getty Images, (TL) Getty Images; **37** (TL) Stacey Newman/Shutterstock, (BL) Corbis, (TR) Gary Crabbe/Enlightened Images/Alamy Images, (BR) Shutterstock; **38** (C) Paul Marcus/Shutterstock, (BL) ©Edward S. Curtis/NGS Image Collection, (TL) ©Victor R. Boswell, Jr./NGS Image Collection, (B) Corbis, (TR) Tom Grundy /Alamy; **39** (C) Mark52/Shutterstock, (T) Corbis; **41** (C) ©Bob Rowan; Progressive Image/Corbis; **42** (BL) AP/Wide World Photos; **43** (T) Nati Harnik/AP Images; **44** (CR) ©Bob Rowan; Progressive Image/Corbis, (BL) inga spence/Alamy Images; **48** (TC) ©Used with permission of the Santa Ynez Band of Chumash Indians. (CR) Shutterstock, (BR) Kippy Spilker/Shutterstock, (TR) ZUMA Press, Inc./Alamy Stock Photo; **49** (T) Luis Sinco/Los Angeles Times/Getty Images, (BR) ©Richard Broadwell/Alamy Images; **50** (C) Inga spence/Alamy Stock Photo, (C) ©Grant V. Faint/Getty Images, (T) ©Randy Mayor/Photolibrary Group, Inc., (TR) Radius Images/Alamy, (BR) Sacramento Bee Staff Photo/NewsCom; **51** (TR) ©Brian Baer/Zuma Press, Inc., (B) ©Compliments of Palm Springs Bureau of Tourism, (B) ©Royalty-Free/Corbis; **52** (CR) ©Brian Baer/Zuma Press, Inc.,

(R) ©Compliments of Palm Springs Bureau of Tourism, (L) Radius Images/Alamy, (CL) Sacramento Bee Staff Photo/NewsCom; **53** (C) North Wind Picture Archives; **55** (T) The Granger Collection, NY; **56** (TR) Courtesy of the John Carter Brown Library at Brown University; **57** (C) stocksnapper/123RF, (TL) Getty Images, (B) The National Park Service, Museum Management Program; **58** (Bkgd) Claudine Van Massenhove/123RF, (CL) ©Robert M. Vera/Alamy Images, (TR) George H.H. Huey/Alamy Stock Photo; **59** (B) ©Bill Freeman/PhotoEdit, (TR) ©Private Collection/Bridgeman Art Library, (BC) ©The Stapleton Collection/Bridgeman Art Library; **60** (TR) ©Stacey Barnett/Shutterstock, (CL, BR) Corbis; **61** (BCL) ©Steve Starr/Corbis, (TR) AKG London Ltd., (CR) Corbis, (BR, BCR) Getty Images, (BCL) National Museum of American History/Smithsonian Institution; **62** (BCL) Inga spence/Alamy Stock Photo, (TR) 1978.008 W/22q/P2:7—PIC/©Courtesy of the Bancroft Library, University of California, Berkeley, (BR) Henry A. Barrios/The Californian/NewsCom; **63** (BL) Chon Kit Leong/Alamy Stock Photo, (BL) ©County of Inyo, Eastern California Museum, (TR) Paul Fearn/Alamy Stock Photo, (BR) Chon Kit Leong/Alamy Stock Photo;

Unit 3: 67 (C) Bridgeman Art Library; **68** (C) The Granger Collection, NY; **69** (TL) Sir Francis Drake, 1581 (miniature) Hillard, Nicholas (1547-1619) (studio 0f)/National Portrait Gallery, London, UK/Photo©Christie's Images/Bridgeman Art Library; **70** (TR) 1995.012—PIC/©Courtesy of the Bancroft Library, University of California, Berkeley, (CR) Corbis, (T) Getty Images; **71** (C) ©David Young-Wolff/PhotoEdit, (CR) ©Ted Streshinsky/Corbis, (L) Paul Sakuma/©Associated Press; **73** (C) Ed Young/Design Pics Inc/Alamy Stock Photo; **74** (CR) Nancy Richmond/Image Works; **75** (B) Uladzik Kryhin/Shutterstock, (TR) SuperStock; **77** Sergio Pitamitz/Robert Harding/NewsCom; **78** (BR) Everett Historical/Shutterstock; **79** (TR) Klotz/123RF, (L) ©Museum of Ventura County; **80** (TR) Corbis, (TC) SuperStock; **81** (CR) ©Underwood Photo Archives/SuperStock;

Unit 4: 85 (C) ©Spencer Grant/PhotoEdit; **86** (BR) ©Day Williams/Photo Researchers, Inc., (BL) ©Karl Kost/Alamy, (BL) ©Warner J. Bertsch/Photoshot; **87** (C) ©Ruth Wallach/University of Southern California Library, (C) The Granger Collection, NY; **88** Alaska State Library; **89** Kali9/E+/Getty Images;

Credits